"We all know leadership transitions can leave things in the lurch, or launch the mission forward. What m̲ḁ̲k̲e̲s̲ t̲h̲e̲ understanding what makes the diff[...] right. Gary Johnson has provided [...] elp leaders navigate through a change a[...] ep desire to be part of a successful succe[...], Gary has mapped out a thoughtful, God-honoring process every conscientious leadership team can use. If you want to plan for an effective leader-shift, read this book!"

Ben Cachiaras, Senior Pastor
Mountain Christian Church,
Joppa, MD

"Death, taxes and succession. These are the three inevitabilities for all leaders. Gary Johnson has found an engaging way to assure us that hope and anticipation can replace denial and despair when it comes to our own succession transition. If you sense you are close to the end of your 'shelf life' and hope to finish well, this book should move to the top of your reading list."

Larry Winger, CEO
Provision Ministry Group

"As a strong advocate for strategic thinking and planning, I applaud this work. Dr. Johnson is addressing a pivotal subject within the evangelical camp. With tumultuous change upon us in America, the continuity of Christian leadership from one generation to another is vital. The why, the how, and the when of succession planning are subjects this book willingly and wisely promotes. He is to be commended for identifying the providence of God and the plans of men as the twin pillars of leadership legacy."

Dr. Keith H. Ray, President
Lincoln Christian University

"This is a timely book that deserves a wide reading. With a direct style and biblically-informed insight, Gary Johnson reminds us that leaders don't own our churches and other organizations; the people and the work belong to God. We are merely his stewards for a season. May God give us the humility and courage to carry out healthy leadership hand-offs so the work will go on without hindrance and God's people will never be "like sheep without a shepherd" (Numbers 27:17)."

Dr. David Faust, President
Cincinnati Christian University

"For nearly two and a half decades Gary Johnson has been putting on a clinic in courageous church leadership, inspiring local pastors like me around the globe. Once again Gary forges new ground by inviting us to join him on his own personal journey for an insider's look at the always delicate, often fumbled, and high stakes world of pastoral transitions."

Gene Appel, Senior Pastor
Eastside Christian Church
Anaheim, CA

*"Gary Johnson's book, **Leader><Shift**, is readable, provocative and an invaluable resource for church leaders today. I particularly like the practical, contemporary illustrations drawn from the secular and church world. Had Gary's book been around when I stepped down following a 40-year tenure as Senior Minister at Southeast Christian Church, I would have made it mandatory reading for our leadership team."*

Bob Russell, Retired Senior Minister
Southeast Christian Church
Louisville, Kentucky

"I have witnessed many serious, damaging, and fatal outcomes resulting from failure to identify, apply and execute leader><shift

scriptural principles when "changing the guard" in many organizational types, styles, and structures. I believe this book identifies and details application of these scriptural principles to assure a successful leader><shift in your situation."

Ethan Jackson,
Corporate CEO

"From his years of effective ministry and leadership in the church, Dr. Gary Johnson has hit a "home run" when it comes to the critical topic of 'transitions' in the church. I highly recommend Gary's work to any leader or leadership team looking for wise and discerning direction from an experienced ministry veteran."

Dr. David Roadcup
Professor of Christian Ministries
Cincinnati Christian University

"My daughter was on the relay track team and she always said the teams most vulnerable time was at the start and when the baton was passed. The same could be said of church leadership. Leader><Shift is a valuable resource to coach a congregation through transitions of leadership and avoid stumbling at such crucial moments."

James Riley Estep Jr., Ph.D.; Dean
School of Undergraduate Studies
Lincoln Christian University

"Every living organism, including the local church, experiences change; with leadership transition being one of the most critical. Yet all too often this most vital process is embarked upon without the thoughtful, prayerful, and well-resourced attention it deserves. Leader><Shift calls us to pause, think, and observe God's role for His Kingdom's leaders and the biblical pattern for passing the mantle from one leader to the next."

David Pace, President
Kairos Legacy Partners

"As a sixty-something church leader thinking about retirement, this book came at the perfect time for me! Gary (who has also begun the process of succession planning at the church he serves) takes a straightforward, unsentimental look at the need for ministers (and other ministry leaders) to move on when their "shelf life" has expired. If ministers and elders and ministry boards will read and heed this book, much potential heartache can be avoided when it's time for the person at the top to retire."

Mark Taylor, Editor/Publisher
Christian Standard

"Leader><shift will quickly become essential reading for any leader or organization that is considering or in the process of making a leadership transition. Actually, it should be considered a must read for anyone who is leading and desires to finish well. It is readable, practical and insightful. Most of all, it reveals the profound truth of God's Word through the Bible."

Greg Nettle
President of Stadia Global Church Planting

"What a necessary read for any leader who cares deeply about the future of the church! Gary's outstanding treatment of the subject of succession is well developed and presented. Weaving together Biblical examples and principles along with contemporary illustrations and quotes makes this a most engaging encounter for those who desire to transition well. Gary's calls for us to "pause" are well-placed and require the reader to crucify ego for Christ's cause. Many thanks for Gary's experience, wisdom, insights and challenge as we press on for the name of Christ."

Steve White, Senior Minister
Plainfield Christian Church; Plainfield, IN

"Gary Johnson is not only a skilled researcher and writer, he is passionate about this subject of transition in ministry. While he has invested energy in Kingdom work around the globe, his ministry heart beats for the local church. This book is a tremendous resource not only for lead pastors who are contemplating retirement or shifts in ministry, but also for volunteer leaders in the local church who must oversee those transitions and help the congregation embrace the changes. In an ever changing business world, the Church should be the one to set the standard on how such transitions are made! Every church leadership team needs to read Gary's book; it will help them prepare for whatever changes the future brings. I truly respect Gary's scholarship but more importantly, as a friend, I am confident in his leadership integrity and love for the church."

Tom Ellsworth, Senior Minister
Sherwood Oaks Christian Church
Bloomington, IN

"Gary has written a sorely needed, immensely insightful and user-friendly resource for leadership transition planning. With his characteristic precision, intentionality and thoroughness, Dr. Johnson unveils a comprehensive template for thinking through the issues and implications of the leadership succession process. He writes as a practitioner humbly dealing with these questions on a practical level and arriving at conclusions that he will ultimately face in his own situation. Perfect for group or individual use, this work will be an indispensable volume for future leader-shift discussions. Leader><Shift will be at the top of my list as I consider the future of my own ministry."

Jeff Faull, Senior Minister
Church at Mt. Gilead
Moorseville, IN

"I know of no person better equipped to write about leadership transition ("leader><shift," as he calls it) than Dr. Gary Johnson. He combines more than thirty years of pastoral experience in a mega-church with a thorough understanding of the scriptures, a keen observation of leadership practice in church and corporate life, and the academic gift of research learned through extensive academic

preparation. *Anyone involved in leadership, whether a practitioner or a follower, can access the central message of the book. In the first section of the book, "The Preliminaries," Gary establishes the need for congregations and para-church organizations to have a transition plan from one leader to another. He demonstrates both positive and negative examples of transition plans both in the church and the corporate world. In following chapters he provides practical suggestions for organizations to construct successful processes of leadership change. In addition to his lively writing style, the frequent graphics help readers to follow the main development of the chapters. I commend the book to congregations, organizations, and individuals contemplating "leader><shift." As one not far from such a "shift," I plan to take careful heed of his sage advice."*

Dr. Gary Weedman, President
Johnson University

"Distilled from decades of thoughtful experience and excellent service, Gary provides a much needed resource TCMII plans to use. A carefully constructed way to help us pass the baton successfully for even greater ministry impact beyond us. Please pass the word and take advantage of this tool to maximize Kingdom resources!"

Tony Twist, PhD, D.Min.; President
TCM International Institute
Heiligenkreuz, Austria

*"When facing a transition in leadership, any organization must decide soon enough to avoid decay. Gary's book, **Leader><Shift** becomes a tutorial on turning succession into a healthy celebration for any organization. Passing the baton, transitioning, succession, whatever description we choose, is all about knowing when to take a side step and diminish our influence. Gary's book on the topic can help avoid catastrophes in an inevitable experience."*

Stan Endicott, Founding Partner
The Slingshot Group

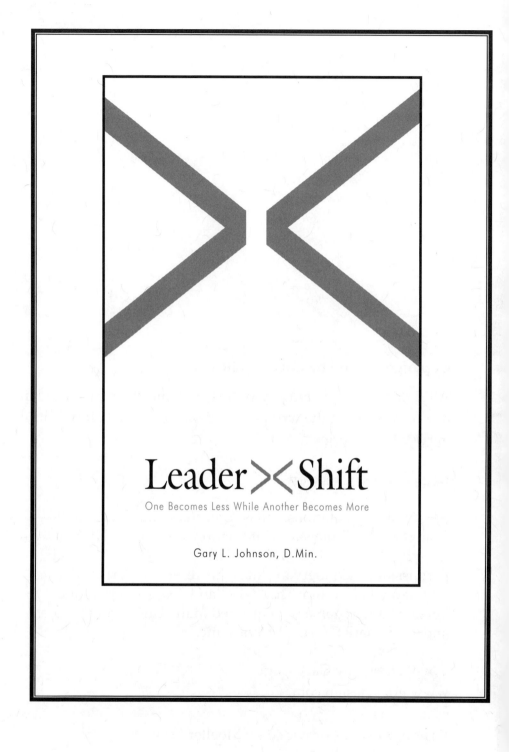

Leader ✕ Shift

One Becomes Less While Another Becomes More

Gary L. Johnson, D.Min.

Dedicated

to my sons, Jared and Aaron, and to their generation,
who I pray, will lead the Church and advance the Kingdom of God
in ways I only dreamed of doing.

Acknowledgments

My sincere and heartfelt thanks to:

my wife, Leah, for her constant encouragement;
the Elders and staff of The Creek for their invaluable teamwork;
the people of the Creek for their unfailing support; and to
Jim Estep, Gary Gogis and Chuck Moeller, for their instrumental help
in producing *Leader><Shift.*

Foreword

The church in America declines substantially, many mega churches continue to thrive. More and more churches are reaching benchmark numbers of 2k, 5k, 10k, or multiples thereof. This is no accident. It is the deliberate result of decades of strategic investment by key leaders. Like never before in the history of the church, we know how to build institutional giants. Our programs are more focused, marketing more shrewd, communication more clear, and networks more sophisticated. We are postured well for growth.

However, there is a black hole in church leadership: Transition Strategy. What we don't know how to do is transition from first generational leaders to second generational successors. It's not that we have no theory; it's that we have few models to follow in churches where the stakes are the highest because of the church's influence and visibility. For every success story like Southeast Christian Church there are multiple tales of devastation like the Crystal Cathedral.

This conversation about leadership transition is overdue and desperately needed. Dr. Johnson has leveraged his wisdom in this addition to a thin body of literature on transitions. His book *Leader>< Shift* is designed to start the conversation in the church. It is a welcome foray into a complex and largely ignored discussion that has massive consequences for our most influential churches in the very near future. Just as we have shared wisdom on sermon preparation, staff building, program strategies, and curriculum development, it is now time to start talking in tandem about how to posture a younger generation of supremely talented pastors for longevity in leadership.

Mark E Moore, Ph.D.
Teaching Pastor
Christ's Church of the Valley,
Peoria, Arizona

Table of Contents

PREFACE

Context Before Content

We need to take time to think. Thomas Edison did. Some years ago, when our family toured his winter home in Fort Myers, Florida, we were shown a dock where Edison would sit fishing for hours. The guide told us that when the venerable inventor was fishing, no one—not even Mrs. Edison—was allowed to step foot on the dock. He wanted to be left alone. A colleague once questioned Edison as to why he never caught any fish, and the inventor confessed that he never baited his hook. Why? Edison did not want to be bothered by the fish. He just wanted time to sit and think.

That is the purpose of this book. It is intended to help us think; particularly about a matter that is given too little thought or consideration—and that being leader><shift. Many of us experience a leader><shift when a long tenured leader transitions out and a successor arrives. As I write this, I am on a sabbatical and have been given time to prayerfully think about the pending transition that will happen in my life when a new senior minister will lead Indian Creek Christian Church (The Creek). For more than thirty years, I've served as a senior minister, and in these past few years, succession planning has been weighing on my mind. Perhaps like me, you are facing a similar change. It is my hope that this book may help you and your leadership team to think through the myriad of issues involved in making an effective transition. The material in this book targets the leader><shift of long tenured ministers, yet its

1

content is also applicable to parachurch ministries, as well as organizations and individuals anticipating leadership transitions.

While in college or seminary, you may have taken a course in hermeneutics, the science of biblical interpretation. One of the essential rules to correctly interpreting Scripture is "context before content." A student of the Word must first establish the context of a passage before dealing with its content. In the same manner, before reading the content of this book, it's necessary to establish the context in which it is written.

Typically, when a pastor or leader prepares to retire after a lengthy and effective tenure, he and the leadership team will focus primarily on finding his replacement. They approach this task with singular intent, and that being to locate a new senior minister. Yet, effective transitions are not limited to finding a new pastor. If we are focused solely on finding a successor to a long-term, respected senior minister without first establishing a plan and implementing a process, we will likely fail in making an effective leader><shift. This issue is complex and multifaceted; involving not one, but a number of significant issues; such as a plan, a process, and a person. So, this book is divided into four primary parts: The Preliminaries (introductory issues), The Plan, The Process and The People. Pastoral succession is the deliberate and intentional transfer of leadership authority from one individual to another. Parts two and three of this book make us think of succession as a planned process. We first develop the succession plan through collaborative thought, discussion and prayer. Once completed, we move from our idea stage to its implementation by beginning the succession process.

Little has been said on this issue. Only a few books are in print. Some articles have appeared in periodicals. Seminars and webinars are beginning to address necessary transitions. There appears to be a proverbial itch that is just now beginning to be scratched. To that end, the context of this book is simply to help leaders think through succession in light of their setting. Every church is a living entity with its own culture, spiritual DNA, and historical journey. When it comes to making this significant change, what works in one congregation will not necessarily work in another. What works in one organization is not guaranteed to work for another. So the focus of this book is to help you think—and ask—vital questions that will lead to a more effective transition.

 Interspersed throughout the book is the image of a pause button. This symbol serves as a reminder to 'push pause' and to think through questions that are raised in reference to various succession issues. The questions are for both individual and team use. Dealing with pertinent questions enables you and your leadership team to think of how this necessary ending can occur more effectively.

As well, biblical principles appear throughout this book. The Scriptures describe several leadership transitions from which we have much to learn. Though we have read these passages over and again throughout the years, it may be that we did not read them with the express purpose of discovering insights to assist us in making a leader><shift. One of the most

important scriptural principles in the time of succession is this: one becomes less while another becomes more. Not only will you often read of this principle, but you will see it every time you come across the word leader><shift. The symbols >< between the words leader and shift are not mathematical, but musical. The > symbol represents *decrescendo*, meaning to become less loud; whereas the symbol < represents *crescendo*, meaning to increase in volume. For a transition in leadership to happen effectively, the exiting leader must willingly become "less loud" in his leadership authority. His voice of authority should be heard less often, while his successor's voice should become all the louder and more often heard by the team he is beginning to lead. This scriptural principle is at the very heart of an effective, God-honoring succession.

Football enthusiasts will long remember when NFL officials went on strike in the fall of 2012. Replacement referees became popular targets of sports reporters and talk-show hosts. Claims of incompetent officiating came to a head when the Green Bay Packers played the Seattle Seahawks. When the Seahawks attempted a touchdown pass, it was intercepted by Green Bay—only for the ball to be wrestled out of the hands of the Green Bay player by the intended Seahawk receiver. There in the end-zone, one replacement ref extended his hands skyward, declaring it a touchdown; while his colleague stood next to him and crossing his hands in front of him, declaring the play incomplete. It was quite a sight, and the video went viral! Throughout their short three-month stint, the replacement refs struggled to make the right calls in keeping with league rules. We do the same. As leaders, we struggle with making the right calls when it comes to effective

4

transitions. All too often, we forget to play by God's rules. Biblical principles must be given serious consideration when we develop a succession plan, implement the process, and attempt to find the right person as a successor.

Finally, each chapter title states a reality that we must grasp. All too often, leaders live in a state of denial when it comes to making this necessary ending. We delay the inevitable. We avoid having essential conversations. To that end, we must grasp the multi-faceted—and sometimes harsh—realities that accompany leadership transitions.

Friend, take time to think. Even before reading this book, think about others who could benefit by reading this with you. Though I am writing with my pastoral colleagues in mind, the principles in this book can help any number of people facing a leader><shift. Perhaps your family-owned business is about to be passed to the next generation. If so, this book may help you think through a number of issues. Maybe you lead a school, a not-for-profit organization, a company or a division within a company. Again, this book may cause you to think about an aspect of your future transition that needs to be given serious consideration. Perhaps you could take some time to get away for a few days to read, while pausing often to think. Like Edison, make and take time to think. Whether sitting on the end of a dock fishing, hiking in the mountains, or walking in a park, think through your leader><shift; and like young Samuel, be sure to say, "Speak, Lord, for your servant is listening" (1 Samuel 3:10). Just think.

Part I
The
Preliminaries

Reality #1:
The Days are Seismic

*"When the foundations are being destroyed, what can
the righteous do?"*
Psalm 11:3

While growing up, one of the first lessons we learn of scientific law has to do with an apple falling from a tree. Versions of the story vary greatly, but the fact remains: Sir Isaac Newton (1642-1727) introduced us to the law of gravity. An English physicist and mathematician, Newton has become known the world over for being a pivotal figure in the scientific and industrial revolutions. Yet, another great mind helped introduce the world to the law of gravity. Edmund Halley (1656-1742) was an English astronomer and physicist, who has become known for computing the orbit of a comet later named after him (i.e., Halley's Comet, appearing every seventy-six years). Halley met Newton at Cambridge University in 1684, and was instrumental in convincing the then-hesitant Newton to write and publish a work that scientifically explained the law of gravity. Moreover, Halley corrected the proofs of Newton's book, wrote the preface honoring its author, and even financed the entire project. In 1687, Sir Isaac Newton's landmark work *Principia Mathematica* was published, due much in part to the effort and investment of Edmund Halley.[1]

Newton quickly took to the world stage as a brilliant scientist, while Halley received little to no credit for his key

---

[1] http://www.britannica.com/EBchecked/topic/252812/Edmond-Halley.

7

contribution to this significant work. Not until after his death would Halley receive acclaim, and that in the form of having a returning comet named after him. Still, Halley remained devoted to the further advancement of science, and did not lose sleep over who received the credit and applause for scientific discovery. While Newton became more, Halley was willing to become less.

ONE BECOMES LESS WHILE ANOTHER BECOMES MORE

Sound familiar? It should. This phenomenon is modeled in Scripture. When we study Acts, a shift between leaders (i.e., leader><shift) took place between Barnabas and Paul. Barnabas was the key leader earlier in Acts, particularly when the Jerusalem church sent him to Antioch to establish a work there (Acts 11:22f). Once he arrived in Antioch, Barnabas planted the church and then went to Tarsus to look for Paul, bringing him to Antioch to help disciple the believers. Barnabas was the lead-servant of the Antioch church while Paul assisted him. Yet, it wasn't long before a leader><shift took place. In Acts 15:39, after a sharp dispute between Barnabas and Paul over John Mark, Barnabas took the rejected John Mark and sailed for their home in Cyprus, and in that moment, he sailed away from the scene of leadership in the first-century church. Barnabas was no longer the key leader in the early church; Paul was. Barnabas became less while Paul became more.

In Acts 20:17f, Paul sent for the Elders of the church at Ephesus. He met with them to tender his resignation as their preacher. Then, in his first letter to Timothy—his adopted son in the faith—Paul told him to "stay there in Ephesus" (1

8

Timothy 1:3) as Timothy was serving that church as their new preacher. Paul became less while Timothy became more. A leader><shift took place.

The same leader><shift happened between John the Baptist and Jesus. First-century Jews thought John was the Messiah, but he consistently deflected any attention in this regard. He knew that he was the forerunner of Christ, preparing for the Messiah's arrival on the scene. In speaking about Jesus, John the Baptist said, "He must become greater; I must become less" (see John 3:30). A leader><shift took place.

In the Old Testament, Moses became less while Joshua became more. In Numbers 27:12-23, Joshua was selected by God as the successor to Moses. God instructed Moses, "Give him some of your authority so the whole Israelite community will obey him" (verse 20). A leader><shift took place. While still alive, King David appointed his son, Solomon, to be the king (see 1 Kings 1:28-48). Solomon became more while David became less. A leader><shift took place.

Can we see a pattern? Do we recognize a biblical principle at work? The truth of the matter is this: leaders change places. They always have in the past, they do so in the present, and they will in the future. Leader><shifts occur when one leader exits and a new leader arrives. A shift among leaders is common in the corporate board room, on university campuses, on military bases, and in the halls of Congress. Moreover, leader><shifts are a normal part of the Christian community, and in particular, there comes a time when a long tenured senior minister hands his leadership position over to another. As in the case of Isaac Newton and Edmund Halley, the exiting minister becomes less, while the incoming minister

9

becomes more. Leader><shifts happen, and they are becoming seismic in nature.

Push pause.

What enables or prevents one leader to become more while another becomes less? Have you been or are you now a part of this kind of transition? Are you becoming more or less in the leader><shift?

WHEN FOUNDATIONS ARE BEING DESTROYED

Seismic movement is not limited to the physical shaking of the ground as when an earthquake strikes. Strong and widespread impact can happen socially within an organization, and that seismic impact is happening currently within many ministries as leader><shifts occur. The seismic dimension of leadership transitions is due largely in part to the demand for high capacity leaders. Churches and parachurch organizations are facing challenges never before experienced, both within our culture and the global community. If we are to effectively advance the kingdom of God, high capacity leaders are needed.

For example, the size and number of megachurches continue to increase. Research leads us to believe that the megachurch phenomenon is not going away any time soon. Further, large churches with young leaders are rapidly increasing in both size and number. These congregations are wrestling with significant internal issues calling for high capacity leadership: establishing multisite campuses, transitioning to externally focused ministries, becoming intergenerational congregations, etc. Ministry demands are made more difficult as we struggle to grow fully devoted followers of Christ, equip and empower the next generation of Christian leaders, develop authentic community among believers, create life impacting worship experiences, while trying to respond to the needs of the broken and disadvantaged around us. There is an unprecedented need for high capacity leaders to navigate ministries through turbulent times.

Moreover, church leaders face challenges of seismic dimension existing outside of the local church. One such challenge lies in the ever-increasing number of people who are spiritually disconnected. The Pew Research Center reports that growing numbers of Americans have no religious affiliation.

> "The number of Americans who do not identify with any religion continues to grow at a rapid pace. One-fifth of the U.S. public – and a third of adults under 30 – are religiously unaffiliated today, the highest percentages ever in Pew Research Center polling. In the last five years alone, the unaffiliated have increased from just over 15% to just under 20% of all U.S. adults. Their ranks now include more than 13 million self-described atheists and agnostics (nearly 6% of the U.S. public), as well as nearly 33 million people who say they have no particular religious affiliation (14%).[2]

Atheism is enjoying a rise in popularity in our country and beyond. In London, a "church" of and for atheists has actually formed called The Sunday Assembly. This group of atheists gathers together on the first Sunday of the month to

---

[2] http://www.pewforum.org/Unaffiliated/nones-on-the-rise.aspx

sing songs and hear someone speak. Meeting in a deconsecrated church building, this atheist get-together has experienced standing room only crowds.[3]

Seeing that the global community increasingly rejects the Judeo-Christian faith, how will the local church effectively reach these individuals? How will parachurch organizations effectively advance the kingdom of God? High capacity leaders are needed, both now and in the future, to help us develop relevant ministries that close the gap between believers and nonbelievers. If you traveled in London on the underground (i.e., subway), you had to have heard a computer generated voice say, "Mind the gap." The gap is the distance between the subway platform and the entry to the rail car. Every time I heard the strong British accent warning me to "mind the gap," I realized that I need to be mindful of the gap that exists between me and those who are not Christ followers. Moreover, the gap is becoming increasingly large, even to the point of becoming a chasm.

Our culture is less accepting of a Christian worldview. People are quickly offended when the Bible contradicts our culture and the way we live. That contradiction should be of no surprise to anyone because the very source of Scripture is God. The Apostle Paul reminds us that, "All Scripture is God-breathed and is useful for teaching, rebuking, correcting and training in righteousness" (2 Timothy 3:16). It is only logical that something in Scripture should offend someone about something in his or her life—no matter where they live in the world. God and His Word transcend every culture. Opposition

---

[3] http://www.nydailynews.com/news/world/atheist-church-huge-success-london-article-1.1257274

12

to Scripture and all things Christian ever widens the gap between nonbelievers and believers.

Global rejection of Christianity is further intensified by widespread persecution. In his book *Christianophobia: A Faith Under Attack* (Rider, 2012), British journalist Rupert Shortt reports that the persecution of Christians is a growing, worldwide phenomenon. He cites global hot spots where harassment and oppression are commonplace treatment of Christians: Egypt, Burma, Sri Lanka, Vietnam, China, India, and others. Writing for *The Telegraph*, Shortt states:

> "The deeper truth masked by all the ranting – and, it should be added, by the blinkers of many Western secularists – is that Christians are targeted in greater numbers than any other faith group on earth. About 200 million church members (10 per cent of the global total) face discrimination or persecution: it just isn't fashionable to say so."[4]

Shortt is right. What he calls not fashionable, others call politically incorrect. In the minds of nonbelievers, it is politically incorrect to say that record numbers of Christians—the world over—experience discrimination and persecution. Yet, that does not change reality. Christian persecution is widespread—and growing. Even here in the States, Christian persecution is conspicuously present. The media has vilified the Christian faith in recent years, and with increasing intensity. Christians are the brunt of mockery in movies and

---

[4] http://www.telegraph.co.uk/news/religion/9640825/Christians-persecuted-throughout-the-world.html

on television. Christianity is ridiculed in the lyrics of songs. Yitzchok Adlerstein, a rabbi of Orthodox Judaism, asks, "Are Christians the new Jews?"[5] He is of the opinion that Christians have replaced the Jews as the most persecuted people on earth.

> "Christians who study Jewish history learn that for close to two thousand years, even when Jews were not being killed, they were terrorized from cradle to grave. They could not speak their mind or voice opinions about political matters. Anything they said might be used against them with deathly consequences as leadership changed, or rulers changed their minds about protecting 'their' Jews from expulsion or death. Moreover, on the rare occasion when they enjoyed enough protection to speak or act, they knew that they might be endangering their co-religionists elsewhere, and so learned to remain mute even in the face of horrific tragedy. Christians today have learned to keep silent while their hearts are exploding with rage."[6]

Not only does Alderstein accurately describe the harsh reality of life for Christians living abroad, but his words aptly describe life for Christians in America who "have learned to keep silent" for fear of cruel reprisals. These are but a few of the external stresses from our culture and global community that impact the local church and parachurch ministries. When

---

[5] http://www.patheos.com/Jewish/Christians-New-Jews-Yitzchok-Adlerstein-02-21-2013.html
[6] Ibid.

added to the unrelenting, internal pressures faced by ministry leaders, we can immediately see the need for high capacity leaders.

We must face the reality that something seismic is happening within and around the body of Christ. Attitude, beliefs and behavior that defy Christianity shakes and impacts us as never before, just as an earthquake of great magnitude shakes and impacts the ground.

Push pause.
What are unique demands in your cultural setting that demand high capacity leadership? What issues of seismic proportion will your successor face in leading your ministry?

So, first things first. When the foundations are being destroyed, what can Christian leaders do? One response involves succession planning, in that we realize that transitions are not merely about finding the next leader. It is about finding and becoming a high capacity leader because the days in which we live demand that we do so. When a leader><shift occurs, the leader leaving must make way for a new leader with high capacity potential; and in that process, one will have to become less, while another becomes more.

15

Reality #2:
Leaders have a Shelf Life

"There is a time for everything, and a season for every activity under heaven: a time to be born and a time to die..."
Ecclesiastes 3:1-2

He had to push forward. It was a decision that could result in life or death. Others attempted to push forward, and they did die when the planes they flew shook apart at high speed, while others crashed and the brave test pilots died on impact. Not Chuck Yeager. On October 14, 1947, USAF test pilot Chuck Yeager pushed his rocket-propelled Bell X-1 jet to its limits and he broke the sound barrier at Mach 1.05, flying at 45,000 feet. When interviewed about that historic moment, Yeager said,

> "And that's the way the X-1 was. When we got it above Mach one without it flying apart, you can laughingly say now, well I was disappointed because it didn't blow up. But that's not true. You are a little bit surprised that things didn't fly apart, because that's the way you've been sort of thinking. But when it didn't you are relieved."[7]

In the face of fear of the unknown, Yeager did the unthinkable – he pushed forward. Knowing that the experi-

_____

[7]http://www.chuckyeager.com/academy-of-achievement-interview

mental jet in which he flew could fall apart around him, he made the conscious and deliberate decision to push forward. We must do the same. As we near the time in life when our leadership shelf life is beginning to diminish, we must push forward. Even though life as we know it will seem to fall apart around us, we must make a conscious and deliberate decision to push forward knowing that it is time to leave behind a ministry position that we have come to know and love.

Yeager's decision to push forward—speeding past the sound barrier—resulted in a myriad of even greater accomplishments in the field of aviation. Like Yeager, when we push forward with the decision to leave, that decision can be historic in scope for the church or parachurch ministry we serve. Our leaving may launch the ministry into a season of unprecedented growth and advancement—the likes of which it has never before experienced. By pushing forward and leaving behind a long held ministry leadership position, we could actually advance the kingdom of God. So then, first things first: accept the reality that leaders have a shelf life.

KNOWING WE HAVE AN EXPIRATION DATE

An entire industry exists to measure and monitor the shelf life of products; such as food, medicines, personal care items, and more. Products are stamped with an expiration date to alert the consumer that the product will not be fresh or effective past that date. What if we could be "stamped with a date", indicating that we are no longer effective as leaders? If only it were that easy! Still, there are signs indicating when we are nearing the end of our leadership shelf life, such as when ...

- Our influence is no longer felt within the organization we lead.
- Our vision is stale and our ideas are dated.
- Our sense of urgency wanes and our energy is easily depleted.
- Our ability to effectively connect with the next generation is lost.
- Our capacity to adapt to change is a thing of the past.
- Our hunger and thirst for learning is anemic or nonexistent.
- Our desire to retool our leadership skills disappears.
- Our ministry methods have not changed in years.
- Our attitudes about leading indicate that we are cruising along in neutral gear.

Only we can determine our expiration date. Others may try to do so, particularly when we refuse to take an honest and much-needed look at ourselves. Real leaders will admit that there comes a time in life when our best years are behind us, and the best years are ahead for those individuals who will replace us. Face that fact. Man up. Come to grips with the reality that every leader has a shelf life. After all, this fact appears as a biblical principle throughout the Scriptures.

Push pause.
What strikes fear in you, preventing you from pushing forward into a transition? What are other signs indicating that a leader has reached the end of his shelf life? Are any of the above traits evident in your life?

18

Reason with me. There came a time when Moses realized that his best years were behind him and the best years were yet ahead for Joshua, his successor. Moses admitted it before God and the people of Israel.

> "Moses said to the LORD, 'May the LORD, the God who gives breath to all living things, appoint someone over this community to go out and come in before them, one who will lead them out and bring them in, so the LORD's people will not be like sheep without a shepherd.'"[8]

Moses knew the day would come when he would not enter the Promised Land. With every step they took and mile they traveled to the border of Canaan, Moses became increasingly aware that his best days were behind him. He accepted the reality that his leadership had a shelf life. So, with courage and determination, Moses pushed forward and asked God to appoint his successor. He could have thought that life around him would fall apart, but he didn't respond in that manner as a leader. Moses had complete faith and trust in God that He would be faithful in leading the Israelites into the Promised Land. Moses knew that God would provide his successor—and He did.

The same can be said of King David. "When King David was old and well advanced in years" (1 Kings 1:1), Adonijah attempted to take his father's throne, declaring, "I will be king" (v. 5). Adonijah had it all worked out. He had an entourage of

---

[8]Numbers 27:15-17

19

people assisting him – people with political power and position in the administration. But news of Adonijah's attempt to depose his father reached the ailing and aging king; forcing David's hand. He had to act—and quickly. So, David abdicated his throne to his son Solomon. Speaking to his wife, Bathsheba—the mother of Solomon, David said:

> "As surely as the LORD lives, who has delivered me out of every trouble, I will surely carry out this very day what I swore to you by the LORD, the God of Israel: Solomon your son shall be king after me, and he will sit on my throne in my place."[9]

In his old age, David came to the realization that his best years were behind him as king. He took immediate action and fulfilled a promise that he had made to his wife by appointing Solomon the king of Israel in his place. Before the sun set that day, Solomon was sitting on the throne as king. David's best days were behind him; while Solomon's best days were still before him.

The news media continually reminds us that more than 10,000 Baby Boomers are retiring daily and this number will continue for the next two decades. Literally millions of Americans will leave behind their work in the business world, the military, education, politics, sales, health related fields, agriculture and more—including that of Christian ministry. But for many ministers, it is hard to bite the proverbial bullet and retire. In those situations, it would help to admit that leaders have a shelf life. After all, this is the life-cycle

---

[9] 1 Kings 1:29-30

established by God and described by Solomon, that there is a "time to be born and a time to die" (Ecclesiastes 3:2).

Push pause.
Are our best days behind us? If so, how can we tell? If not, could we be wrong and refusing to admit it?

OUR LIFE CYCLE

The biochemist and science fiction author Isaac Asimov (1920-92) said, "Life is pleasant, death is peaceful. It's the transition that troubles me."[10] When we read Ecclesiastes, it appears that aging King Solomon was troubled with the transition he faced as he neared his expiration date. It is more than obvious that Solomon was a miserable man in his autumn years. He wrote Ecclesiastes in the final season of life and looking back on his life, he declared: "Yet when I surveyed all that my hands had done and what I had toiled to achieve, everything was meaningless, a chasing after the wind; nothing was gained under the sun" (see Ecclesiastes. 2:11). Nearing the end of the book, Solomon described the end of his life and what was weighing on his mind. We need to appreciate and understand the rich metaphors that Solomon used to describe his end-of-life misery [note the metaphor interpretation in *italics*].

---

[10]http://www.goodreads.com/quotes/2389-life-is-pleasant-death-is-peaceful-it-s-the-transition-that-s

Ecclesiastes 12:1-5

1 Remember your Creator in the days of your youth before the days of trouble come and the years approach when you will say, "I find no pleasure in them"— [*appealing to younger people to turn to and remain faithful to God before they grow old with many regrets in old age like him*] 2 before the sun and the light and the moon and the stars grow dark, and the clouds return after the rain; [*recurring depression in old age*] 3 when the keepers of the house tremble, [*legs are weak, shaking*] and the strong men stoop, [*shoulders and back become stooped*] when the grinders cease because they are few, [*teeth are falling out*] and those looking through the windows grow dim; [*failing vision*] 4 when the doors to the street are closed [*no interest in going anywhere*] and the sound of grinding fades; [*hearing loss*] when people rise up at the sound of birds, [*trouble sleeping*] but all their songs grow faint; [*voices becoming weaker*] 5 when people are afraid of heights and of dangers in the streets; [*increased fears*] when the almond tree blossoms [*hair turns gray*] and the grasshopper drags itself along [*difficulty in walking*] and desire no longer is stirred. [*no sexual desire*] Then people go to their eternal home and mourners go about the streets. [*italics mine*]

Our God-ordained cycle of life has an end, and as we near that end, we can be miserable and troubled like King Solomon or we can have a strong finish. The transition doesn't have to be troubling, whether we are leaving this life or our position of leadership.

We enter into life and exit from life. It is the ebb and flow of life, an inescapable rhythm that involves a handoff. When we die, we hand off to those coming behind us a number of things: our money, our homes, and our property; that is, if we have any of that left. Yet, even before we die, there are hand offs that happen in life. It may be that you have a business or a farm that you will hand off to someone. For those in ministry leadership, there will come a time when we will hand off our roles and responsibilities to another person. Keep thinking with me.

In his book *Necessary Endings*, clinical psychologist Henry Cloud describes how endings can be a step to something better. He believes that many people are hesitant to bring about necessary endings, yet Cloud advises people to adopt endings as an ordinary part of life.

> "Make the concept of endings a normal occurrence and a normal part of business and life, so you expect and look for them instead of seeing them as a problem. If you really believe that pruning, seasons, and life cycles are as real as gravity, you will not have to be talked into them; and you will always be looking for them."[11]

Far too often, we avoid the necessary ending of our leadership role, and we then fail to execute an effective transition. As a result, the opportunity for the succession of a gifted, high capacity leader may be lost and the misery of failed

---

[11]Henry Cloud, *Necessary Endings: The Employees, Businesses, and Relationships That All of Us Have to Give Up to Move Forward* (New York: Harper Collins, 2010), p. 87.

transitions may become a repeating pattern. We must accept the cold, harsh reality that a necessary ending must happen in each of our lives someday, and when that time comes, we must willingly vacate the lead chair to another. Our best days will be behind us and our successor's best days will yet lie before him. After all, every leader has a shelf life.

Push pause.
Have you been a part of a handoff; perhaps in your family or at work? What were some of the emotions associated with the handoff? Are necessary endings an ordinary or problematic part of your ministry culture—and why?

Reality #3:
Much is at Stake

"Now it is required that those who have been given a trust must prove faithful."
1 Corinthians 4:2

We hear of it in the news all too often. Time after time, trust is broken. In May, 2010, then Indiana Congressman Mark Souder resigned after admitting to an affair with a member of his staff. Though we have heard of many politicians and people in other positions of influence having a moral lapse, Souder's was different than most because he agonized over what he had done. In more than a dozen e-mails with **WORLD** magazine, Souder reflected on his infidelity.

> "I prayed multiple times a day, sang hymns with emotions and tears, felt each time that it wouldn't happen again, read the Bible every morning .... So how in the world did I have a torrid—which is an accurate word—many-year affair? How could I compart-mentalize it so much? My sin, while forgiven, is greater in that God put me in a position of public trust, so I deserve whatever criticism I receive."[12]

Though Mark Souder did the unthinkable, he actually did that which was remarkable—he admitted that he broke a

---

[12]Emily Belz, "Lessons from a Broken Man," WORLD magazine (6-19-10).

trust that had been given to him. In addition to breaking the trust of his wife, he broke the trust given to him by the people of Indiana's third congressional district when they elected him to office. As a political leader, Mark Souder was given a significant trust, but he did not remain faithful. In much the same way, as leaders in the body of Christ, we have been given a trust and we must prove to be faithful. Whether we lead the local church or a parachurch ministry, the Scriptures call us to be faithful.

There are a number of congregations that have been found faithful to the trust given them. When making their leader><shift, they did so effectively and for a variety of reasons. Their stories are encouraging in that we know succession planning can be successful. Among churches of all sizes, there are congregations that have transitioned well following the retirement of a long tenured pastor. Moreover, we know of megachurches that have transitioned effectively, such as Southeast Christian Church in Louisville, Kentucky. When founding Pastor Bob Russell retired, the church was nearing twenty thousand in worship services and an effective transition would be essential to maintain their increasing momentum. After carefully developing a plan, the leaders of Southeast executed a flawless transition when one pastor became less and another became more. To know more of the specifics, the Southeast story is told in Bob Russell's book *Transition Plan* with Bryan Bucher (Ministers Label Publishing, 2010).

Push pause.

What ministries are you aware of that have completed an effective succession? Likewise, what ministries are you familiar with that have failed at making a succession? Why do some succeed and some fail?

WHEN TRUST IS BROKEN

In times of transition, fulfilling a trust can be far from reality. Case in point, consider the Crystal Cathedral. Over the years, the ministry of the Reverend Robert H. Schuller had an impact that was felt both locally and globally, particularly through its televised program "The Hour of Power." Millions of people toured the campus of the Crystal Cathedral and thousands of people were members of this Reformed Church of America congregation. Yet, in spite of what appeared to be healthy and growing on the outside, a diseased ministry was spreading on the inside.

The succession plan called for the ministry to pass from father to son. The elder Robert Schuller retired and his son, Dr. Robert A. Schuller led the ministry from 2006-08. The transition failed. In a candid, public admission; the younger Robert Schuller shared how he had returned to the Cathedral to help his father lead the ministry as the elder Schuller was struggling. By 2006, the founding pastor had a difficult time following a worship program and had to be prompted by others. By 2008, Schuller was of the opinion that his father was no longer able to lead and that he needed to resign from all responsibilities at the Cathedral. But, he did not do so.

Robert Schuller said that his father stayed too long because he did not have a plan for retirement, sharing that his father should have had an annual salary that would have enabled him to retire. In addition, the succession plan failed because of sibling rivalry with his sisters. Still, the elder Schuller controlled who his successor was, and in 2008, he removed his son from that position.[13]

Since that time, the Crystal Cathedral has suffered great loss. Media reports describe of how they sold their multimillion dollar campus, relocated to another facility, filed bankruptcy and are embroiled in litigation. The Crystal Cathedral's iconic glass structure was sold for a staggering $57.5 million to the Roman Catholic Diocese of Orange (County). Sheila Schuller Coleman was appointed senior pastor of the church, but later resigned because of an adversarial relationship with the ministry's Board of Directors. Founding Pastor Robert Schuller and his wife also resigned from the board, a decision that followed the termination of another daughter and son-in-law from the staff of the Crystal Cathedral.[14]

The Crystal Cathedral congregation is divided. Some are following Sheila Schuller Coleman, who has started a new church. Others are staying with the Cathedral, but moving to a new location where the grandson of the Crystal Cathedral's founder is the lead pastor. The Reverend Bobby Schuller is leading the Cathedral, which relocated to the Shepherd's Grove.[15]

---

[13] Webinar on Succession Planning, featuring Dr. Robert A. Schuller, Leadership Network, 3/26/13.
[14] http://latimesblogs.latimes.com/lanow/2012/03/crystal-cathedral-divided-as-schuller-leave-changes-planned.html
[15] http://www.crystalcathedral.org/

Think for a moment. How many people invested their lives in the Crystal Cathedral? How many millions of hours of time were given by thousands of volunteers over the years? How many people sacrificed financially to give literally millions of dollars since 1955 – all in hopes of advancing the kingdom of God through this ministry? The aging Robert H. Schuller should have realized that his leadership had a shelf life, and that his best years were behind him. He—and the leaders of the ministry—should have taken responsible action to formulate a transition plan and set it into place. It would appear from recurring reports in the media that leaders of the Crystal Cathedral failed to make an effective transition. They had been given a trust. Did they prove faithful?

Much the same happened to another nationally recognized ministry. First Baptist Church of Dallas, Texas, had been led for nearly one hundred years by only two pastors: Dr. George W. Truett and Dr. W. A. Criswell. First Baptist was one of the most powerful protestant churches in America during the twentieth century, boasting a membership exceeding 25,000 and a multifaceted ministry involving a K-12 Christian school system, a Bible college, and extensive ministry to the homeless—all housed on a campus in downtown Dallas covering five city blocks.

Criswell became the pastor of First Baptist in 1944 and intended to stay past his fiftieth anniversary, when he was well into his eighties—that is, according to his then appointed successor, Dr. Joel Gregory. In his tell-all book *Too Great a Temptation: The Seductive Power of America's Super Church*, Gregory described a painful situation that was highly dysfunctional. He had been hired to become Criswell's successor, but what he thought would be a three month transition turned out to be an indefinite transition of many years. In his short tenure of twenty-two months, Gregory was given little—if any—information as to what was actually happening. He was sharing preaching responsibilities with Criswell and managing staff. Yet, it was a vexing situation to Gregory because he finally came to a painful conclusion.

> "I had accepted the call thinking that I would be the pastor of the church. In reality, I was there to extend the tenure of W.A. Criswell. I had been told there would be a transition within 'a few months'; there was no transition at all...The state and actual reason for my departure was the dysfunctional transition with the previous pastor of forty-eight years, the legendary Dr. W.A. Criswell. I had been promised a transition of 'a few months.' After two years, he announced his intention to remain for two more. I quit."[16]

Criswell had made a decision—and a promise—to leave the church once his replacement had been chosen so that he could transition and serve in leadership at Criswell College. That never happened. He stayed at First Baptist and fulfilled his long held dream of serving the church for fifty years, when Dr. W. A. Criswell was the celebrated age of eight-four. When is enough enough? Did Criswell fail to come to grips with the fact that his leadership had a shelf life? Moreover, when Gregory was called to serve First Baptist, the church had lost

---

[16] Joel Gregory, *Too Great a Temptation: The Seductive Power of America's Super Church.* (Fort Worth, TX: The Summit Group, 1994), pp. 4, xiii.

thousands of members to other Dallas area churches. Giving was down significantly and the church was millions of dollars in debt. Can we stay too long? Can we harm the local church or ministry? Yes and yes. When we do so, we fail at keeping a God-given trust.

Nationally known ministries fail at transition, and so do ministries that are lesser known. Yet, we know them. We can name them by name. Regretfully and all too often, our friends and colleagues are involved in painful, failed transitions. For a variety of reasons, the local church or parachurch ministry ineffectively hands the baton of leadership to the next leader. When that baton of responsibility is dropped, ministry momentum is lost. People leave and they take resources of time, talent and treasure with them. Opportunities to advance the kingdom of God are lost, sometimes indefinitely. Though we have been given a trust, we do not always prove faithful.

Push pause.
When we see trust broken and the Bride bruised, do we become angry? When we witness failed transitions because of out of control egos, do we become angry? If these failed ministries involve our friends, should we confront them in conversation? If so, how?

THE ELEPHANT IN THE MIDDLE OF THE ROOM
Much is at stake when there are leader><shifts. The real issue looming before us is more significant than the larger than life personalities either leaving or arriving during transitions.

Yet few people want to talk about the proverbial elephant in the middle of the room.

In their book *The Elephant in the Boardroom: Speaking the Unspoken about Pastoral Transitions*, Carolyn Weese and J. Russell Crabtree are determined to discuss openly what many others are just as determined to deny.

> "…it is important to make the point that struggle around leader transition is almost all emotional and/or spiritual. We are afraid of the topic and therefore do not talk about it. We do not talk about it, and therefore we are afraid of it. The fact that we avoid such issues, make discussion of them taboo, reward silence, punish honesty, and put systems in place that perpetuate dysfunction is a spiritual issue."[17]

Far too many leaders refuse to directly and deliberately address this issue, and for a variety of reasons. For many, there is a struggle with fear of the unknown. When a beloved, long term leader leaves the key leadership position of a church or parachurch organization, constituents fear the worst. In the case of a local church, there is a fear that a large number of people will see the leader><shift as their prime opportunity to look for another church to attend. When there is a loss of people, contributions of both time and money will occur — leaving the local church in a difficult and challenging situation. Based on their experience, Weese and Crabtree estimate a

---

[17]Carolyn Weese and J. Russell Crabtree. *The Elephant in the Boardroom: Speaking the Unspoken About Pastoral Transitions* (San Francisco, CA: Jossey-Bass, 2004), p. 25.

fifteen percent drop in both worship attendance and general fund giving.[18]

This fear of loss is more than feeling; it is a fact. Following the death of Apple cofounder Steve Jobs on October 5, 2011, the venerable company experienced significant loss in the financial market, reaching in excess of $290 billion in shareholder wealth. An article appeared in the *USA TODAY* Money section, stating: "The Apple stock crash is reaching a historic order of magnitude, shaking the faith of investors who piled on in large part on Jobs' showmanship."[19] Though there are a number of reasons why a company's stock value can drop, this article attributes Apple's financial downturn on one primary cause—the death of Steve Jobs. In recent years, when Apple struggled after Steve Jobs gave his CEO position to another individual, he returned to lead Apple with energy, vision and a host of new ideas. Yet, after Jobs died and his absence was felt permanently, Apple has become just another stock. Downturns do happen when a beloved, long term leader is gone. Such fears are well founded.

Fear of the unknown not only keeps an organization's constituency in denial, such fear can paralyze the departing leader. When leaving the key leadership position of the local church or ministry organization, an exiting leader can fear that transition. He can assume that the organization will be left in a worse condition without him, and to prevent that from happening, the leader remains in a state of denial and silence. The departing leader refuses to discuss his eventual departure,

---

[18]Ibid., p. 30.
[19]Mark Krantz, "Leadership Loss Shocks Stock", *USA Today Money*, 4/19/13.

and in some instances, forbids it to be discussed. Again, Weese and Crabtree observed:

> "...Jesus was candid and forthright about His arrival on the scene and equally transparent regarding His departure. Although the people on both ends tried to deny this reality, Jesus was unrelenting in His focus. In the church today, the situation is often reversed. Members try to face the reality of a leadership change, while the leader denies it... When it comes to pastoral transition, leaders often stop leading."[20]

Michael LaMonica, an elder at Willow Creek Community Church in Barrington, Illinois, spoke of pastoral transition during Leadership Network's webinar on succession planning. LaMonica stated that some church leadership teams need to initiate this conversation with the exiting pastor, and when doing so, they must communicate authentic care for the individual. In reference to founding Pastor Bill Hybels, LaMonica shared that Hybels cannot be lectured about succession planning, but that he must be led there in conversation and that can only happen when a trusted relationship exists with the pastor. With great respect for their pastor, who has led Willow for nearly forty years, the elder team has carefully and strategically initiated the necessary conversations about succession planning.[21]

---

[20]Ibid., p. 14.
[21]Webinar on Succession Planning, featuring Michael LaMonica, Leadership Network, 3/26/13.

So, if you sense the proverbial elephant being in the middle of the room, do something about it. Why? Much is at stake. There is a powerful biblical principle at play in this issue. What matters most is advancing the kingdom of God. After all, we are under a mandate to do so. In the final days of His life, Jesus taught the parable of the talents (see Matthew 25:14-30). In the parable, the master entrusted his servants with his property and then went off on a long journey, only to return and settle accounts with the servants. Those who increased his property were rewarded and affirmed, whereas the servant who maintained the master's property was reprimanded and punished.

Jesus Christ has entrusted us with His kingdom. He is gone from us for an indefinite period of time and will return when least expected, and when He does, He will hold us accountable for what we did—or did not do—with His kingdom. We are to advance His kingdom through the specific ministry we lead, and that will require us to lead with exceptional skill and commitment. To that end, we must admit that each of us has a leadership shelf life, and when the time comes, we must step aside so that another leader can take our place—advancing the kingdom of Jesus Christ in ways we did not or could not accomplish. More is at stake than maintaining our personal income stream or our desire to reach certain accumulated years of service. More is at stake than the personality cult of an exiting or incoming leader. If we fail to execute an effective leader><shift, the local church or parachurch organization can—and will—lose momentum. Moreover, our ministry may give up ground to the evil one for which we fought long and hard. Much is at stake, for it is

required that those who have been given a trust must prove faithful.

Push pause.

Have you spotted an elephant in your leadership team meetings? How and when can you break the silence by initiating conversation about succession planning? Have you considered studying the parable of the talents together? How can your leadership team be on the same page spiritually in that you will all be held accountable for advancing the kingdom of God?

Reality #4:
Stay on Mission

"As the time approached for Him to be taken up to heaven,
Jesus resolutely set out for Jerusalem."
Luke 9:51

Continually swimming in a sea of red ink, the United States Postal Service (USPS) is broke. Losing billions, the USPS faces possible bankruptcy. Recurring losses over recent years exceed billions of dollars. In order to survive, the system is considering the lay-off of postal workers, the closing of post offices, and the increase of postal rates. Even next day delivery is at risk of being discontinued and it may take as long as nine days for your favorite magazine to be delivered to you.[22]

Without a doubt, the USPS has been one of our most important institutions. For decades, the service was our largest public sector employer and it kept people connected during some of the most difficult days in our history. Families separated because of war coveted the moment when letters arrived from home or the war front. The USPS delivered mail by steamboat when roads were yet to be built in our developing nation. The United States Postal Service has been a mainstay in the heart of America.

Yet, technology is changing at a break-neck pace, making it difficult for the USPS to keep pace. Years ago, the fax machine was considered a great threat to the USPS, but even that has been eclipsed by e-mail and other forms of electronic

---

[22] http://www.huffingtonpost.com/2011/12/04/us-postal-service-faces-b_n_1127989.html

communication. Though our postal system is one of the most efficient in the world, the USPS is challenged by competing delivery systems.

Still another institution is struggling to stay current in our rapidly changing culture, that being the Church. A mainstay in the heart of America, the Church is losing ground. In his landmark study of over 200,000 churches, David Olsen's research proved that the American Church is rapidly declining in a number of ways. His book, *The American Church in Crisis*, indicates that "seventy-seven percent of Americans do not have a consistent, life-giving connection with a local church.[23] According to his findings, if the current trends continue, far fewer Americans will be involved in the local church than at any other time in our history. When you Google "how many churches close annually in America," numerous sites estimate that 3,500--4,000 churches close every year, and far fewer new churches are started every year. We are losing ground.

The postal service is in the business of delivering the mail, whereas the Church is in the business of delivering the message of hope found in the resurrection of Jesus Christ from the dead. We are failing to reach people with that message as people are disinterested in Christianity more so than at any time in our past. Like the USPS, the Church appears to be struggling with outdated delivery methods. Yet, could our unhealthy condition be symptomatic of a far greater problem?

---

[23] David T. Olsen, *The American Church in Crisis* (Grand Rapids: Zondervan, 2008), p. 30.

Push pause.
When we go for a doctor's appointment, the nurse takes our vital signs to establish our immediate state of health. What do spiritual vital signs reveal about the current state of health in the American Church? What could be at the root cause of our painful diagnosis?

IN WHAT BUSINESS ARE WE?

As leaders of the local church, we may have forgotten what business we're in today, and that is a most serious problem. The 132 year-old Eastman Kodak Company filed for bankruptcy, largely due to forgetting that it was in the business of photography.[24] Wal-Mart and K-Mart are in the retail business. Cracker-Barrel and McDonalds are in the food business. The NBA and NFL are in the entertainment business. Yet, what is our line of business? First and foremost, the Church is to be in the business of making disciples (i.e., Christ followers) of all people, but are we? Is the church we lead growing numerically? Are we finding the spiritually lost around us, leading them to Christ and then growing them in Christ?

According to Christine Wicker in *The Fall of the Evangelical Nation: The Surprising Crisis Inside the Church* we are failing to accomplish our purpose.

---

[24] http://www.buffalonews.com/business/article715288.ece

"Evangelical Christianity in America is dying. The great evangelical movements of today are not a vanguard. They are a remnant, unraveling at every edge. Look at it any way you like: Conversions. Baptisms. Membership. Retention. Participation. Giving. Attendance. Religious literacy. Effect on culture. All are down and dropping. It's no secret. Even as evangelical forces trumpet their purported political and social victories, insiders are anguishing about their great losses, fearing what the future holds. Nobody knows what to do about it. A lot of people can't believe it. No wonder. The idea that evangelicals are taking over America is one of the greatest publicity scams in history, a perfect coup accomplished by savvy politicos and religious leaders, who understand media weaknesses and exploit them brilliantly."[25]

Wicker's comments are correct. Her findings echo those of Thom and Sam Rainer in their book *Essential Church: Reclaiming a Generation of Dropouts*:

"Most churches are dwindling. Most denominations are not growing. The population in the United States is exploding, recently surpassing the three hundred million mark. But, the church is losing ground. We are in a state of steep decline. ...The American church is dying. Conversions are declining in almost every denomination. Even in some of the more relatively

---

[25] Christine Wicker, *The Fall of the Evangelical Nation: The Surprising Crisis Inside the Church* (New York: Harper One, 2008), p. ix.

40

healthy denominations, conversions to Christianity have stagnated."[26]

The American Religious Identification Survey (ARIS) cites a continual rise in the number of Americans claiming to have no religious affiliation. An article appearing in *USA Today* made the observation: "As our population continues to increase, the number of nonbelievers continues to increase. The numbers reveal the stark truth: the Church has stopped growing."[27]

If our children stopped growing physically, we would go to the doctor and ask, "What's the problem?" After all, the human body has been designed to grow, and if the body does not grow, something is obviously wrong. The same is true of the Church. God has designed the Church to grow numerically with people coming to Christ. Yet, if the church is not growing then something is obviously wrong, and it takes courageous leaders to intentionally ask, "What is wrong here?" That which is wrong could be a misplaced focus. Instead of having a laser-like focus on seeking and saving the lost, the local church may be chasing after a host of less important priorities.

We measure what is important. If our weight is important, we will step on the scales every morning. As we count the worship attendance and the number of new members, we may find that our increase is nothing more than transfer growth. Yet, if our conversion growth is important,

---

[26] Thom Rainer and Sam Rainer. *Essential Church?: Reclaiming a Generation of Dropouts* (Nashville: Broadman & Holman Publishing, 2008), p. 8.
[27] http://www.usatoday.com/news/religion/story/2011-12-25/religion-god-atheism-so-what/52195274/1

church leaders will count the number of baptisms taking place, and they will analyze how people are coming—or not coming—to Christ in their congregation. Moreover, the Christian life is all about transformation. We are called to become fully devoted followers of Jesus Christ, and if we pursue that endeavor, there should be measurable evidence of transformation within the community of believers. After all, we must measure what is important.

What does this have to do with leader><shift? Why is this issue of importance to a change in who leads the local church? Both the exiting and incoming leader must accept and grasp the primary mission of the church. If they do not, they will fail to cast before the congregation a clearly understood, God-honoring vision. While growing up in Michigan, my dad took my brothers and me deer hunting, and in Michigan, hunters can use shotguns or rifles. If a hunter was not a good shot, he would more than likely use a shotgun loaded with pellets. When he pulled the trigger, the pellets would scatter in the direction of the target in hopes of bagging the deer. However, if the hunter was a sure shot, he would use a slug in his rifle and upon pulling the trigger; he would most certainly bag the deer. In leading the church, we should not have a paradigm of differing programs, hoping to somehow impact lives of people—particularly those who do not yet follow Christ. We want to have a single, laser-like focus of our mission, and that is to seek and to save the lost. Nothing matters more to God. The exiting and incoming leaders must grasp this God-honoring truth.

Push pause.

Review your congregation's activities. How do they intentionally pursue people who are not yet followers of Christ? In what ways are your ministry initiatives connecting with people who are far from God?

JESUS ON MISSION

The words are familiar to many of us: "Your mission, should you decide to accept it..." Those were the opening words of each episode of *Mission Impossible*, a television show that aired for nearly ten years, and later inspired a number of movies by the same title. Like the television show, the movies followed the same plot line: a mission that appeared to be absolutely impossible to accomplish was assigned to a secret operative, who could accept or reject the assigned mission.

A mission—that appeared to be absolutely impossible—was accepted by none other than Jesus Christ. It goes like this: God had a dilemma. Being just, God would find each and every person—throughout all of human history—guilty of sin and condemn all humankind to hell. Yet, God abounds in love and His compassion is never-ending. So then, how would God redeem fallen humankind, making eternal life available to every person? Enter to center stage – Jesus Christ, the sinless Lamb of God who takes away the sins of the world. In 1 Peter 1:20, we read that Christ was chosen "before the foundations were laid." This singular truth declares that before God said, "Let there be light," Jesus Christ willingly agreed to come and die for us. He came on a mission, and it was one that He decided to accept. Think of it this way.

43

Lost people are of greatest concern to God. He cares more about lost people than He does about our new buildings and new programs. A myriad of Scripture affirms this fact. God so deeply loved the world that He sent His Son Jesus to save us from our sin (John 3:16). God personally demonstrated the depth of His love for lost people in that while we were yet wallowing in our sin, Christ died for us (Romans 5:8). Even the last verse in Jonah reveals God's compassion for the lost when He asked about Nineveh, "Should I not be concerned about that great city?" (Jonah 4:11). God was not concerned about Nineveh's unemployment rate or rising crime rate. He was concerned about the lost people in Nineveh.

Like father, like son—lost people are of greatest concern to Jesus; so much so that Jesus "did not consider equality with God something to be grasped but made Himself nothing...He humbled Himself and became obedient to death, even death on a cross." (see Philippians 2:6-8) Because we have been made in God's image, lost people should be our greatest concern as we lead His Church. Our mission—should we decide to accept it—is the same as that of Christ Jesus, which is to seek and to save the lost.

Jesus knew His mission. He said it Himself, "The Son of Man has come to seek and to save what was lost" (Luke 19:10). Moreover, Jesus was determined to complete His mission, that being to die on the cross. It was said of Him, "When the time approached for Him to be taken up to heaven, He resolutely set out for Jerusalem" (Luke 9:51). This was the beginning of the end of the earthly life of Jesus Christ. It was then that He began His final journey to Jerusalem as He had a date with death; death on a cross.

Jesus not only knew His mission, but He also protected His mission. Not only was there an appointed time when Jesus had to die (see Matthew 26:18), but He also had to die in a predetermined way—by crucifixion (see John 3:14, 12:30-31). Jesus could not die prematurely, nor could He die by being stabbed, stoned, thrown off the cliff at Nazareth, etc. He had to fulfill the prophesy regarding His death, or had He died in another way on another day other than predetermined by God, Jesus would have been a false prophet and He could not have been our sinless Savior, the Spotless Lamb of God.

Jesus protected His mission in a number of ways. He spoke carefully so as not to inflame the hatred of the Jews towards Him. For example, Jesus referred to Himself as the Son of Man, and not as the Son of God. Had He done so, the Jews would have stoned Him to death on the grounds of blasphemy. As well, Jesus deliberately avoided dangerous places where the Jews were waiting to take His life (see John 7:1, 11:53-54; Matthew 12:14-16). Furthermore, Jesus surrounded Himself with people who were supportive of Him, and they were the same people whom the Jews feared (see Matthew 21:45-46). Even during the final week of His life, Jesus expertly managed all of the details that led to His arrest in the Garden of Gethsemane, His trial, and His execution—all in keeping with the will of God.

Not only did Jesus know and protect His mission; He paid the supreme price of fulfilling His mission. Certainly, there was a physical cost. The horrific suffering at the hands of the Roman executioners is beyond our understanding. All we have to do is watch Mel Gibson's movie *The Passion of the Christ* and cinematography helps us grasp the brutal torture Jesus suffered in completing His mission. And why? He loved us. It was His life for our lives. The Bible says that the wages of sin is death (Romans 6:23). The price of our immoral living is death, but Jesus took and paid that price of eternal life for us. He picked up the tab on our behalf. But that was not the complete cost. Just as music can *crescendo* (i.e., intensify and grow louder), so the suffering of Jesus intensified.

There was an emotional cost in completing His mission. Let's think this through together. Jesus is God. Jesus said, "I and the Father are one" (John 10:30). As well, remember that Jesus is the Creator. In Colossians 1:16, we read, "...all things were made by Him and for Him." Jesus-God, the Creator, was on the cross; and the creatures He made were mocking Him, spitting on Him, striking Him with their fists, stripping Him naked of His clothes, ripping the flesh of His back open by scourging, driving nails through His hands and feet, and thrusting a spear into His side. The creature did that to the Creator, and the Creator allowed it. Why? He loved us—and was willing to let us kill Him so that we could live eternally. How this had to have broken His heart. The emotional cost of fulfilling His mission cannot be calculated.

Yet, the greatest cost of completing His mission was of a spiritual nature. The spiritual suffering of Jesus on the cross eclipsed His physical and emotional suffering. This is the greatest price that He paid for our sins. During His six hours on the cross, something happened in the relationship between Jesus and God, His Father. While He was being nailed to the cross, Jesus said, "Father, forgive them for they do not know what they are doing" (Luke 23:34). At the end of the six hours of suffering on the cross, Jesus said, "Father, into your hands I commit my spirit" and He breathed His last (Luke 23:46). Yet, somewhere between those two statements, Jesus said, "My God, My God, why have You forsaken Me?" (Mathew 27:46). Something happened to their relationship while Jesus was on the cross. We can hear it in the words of Jesus when He said, "Father" then "God" and then back to "Father" before dying. While on the cross, there came a moment when God "laid on Him the iniquity of us all" (Isaiah 53:6) and in that moment, God poured out His full fury and wrath on His Son—wrath that was meant for us! The Father had never treated His Son in this manner before, and this was the "cup" that Jesus had prayed would pass from Him while in Gethsemane. The word "cup" refers to the cup of God's wrath (see Isaiah 51:17, 22; Jeremiah 25:15; Revelation 14:10, 16:19). Jesus did not pray to be spared the cross for it was already determined "before the foundation of the earth was laid" (see 1 Peter 1:20) that He would be our spotless Lamb, dying for our sins. The greatest cost for fulfilling His mission was that he had never before experienced the wrath and rejection of His Father. Jesus died on a certain day, in a certain way, for a certain reason – to pay the penalty of our sin, thus providing us with the gift of eternal life. Mission accomplished.

Push pause.
As leaders, is our mission fuzzy? Do we not understand our primary mission? Once we affirm that it is to bring lost people to Christ, will we protect our mission from every minor distraction and secondary priority? Are we willing to pay the price of pursuing and fulfilling

our mission, even if it means being rejected by the people of the church we are trying to lead?

START WITH WHY

Let there be no confusion, we are leaders, and we are to lead His Church by bringing people to Christ. Strong leaders make for strong churches and strong churches are a stronger threat to the kingdom of darkness. This is at the heart of why we exist.

When the exiting and incoming leaders accept and pursue the mission of the church, a more effective leader><shift can take place. Moreover, when the Elders and executive leadership team pursue this mission with zeal and urgency, leader><shifts will happen with greater ease and effectiveness. Leaders must know their mission, protect their mission, and be willing to pay the price of fulfilling their mission—it's all about "the why."

In his book *Start With Why* (2009; Penguin Group), Simon Sinek has been helping businesses and organizations see the importance of "the why." A few years ago, Simon Sinek presented a brief talk on the learning platform TED.com, presenting what he calls "The Golden Circle." To understand his theory, Sinek drew three concentric circles, two of which were in the largest of the three (see below). In summary, he said that most companies and organizations approach business from the outside by first knowing WHAT they do, then knowing HOW they do business, and with only a few of the people knowing WHY they exist. The majority of their constituents (i.e., management, labor, shareholders, members, etc.) know WHAT products or services they provide, and some of the constituents even know HOW they are provided, but very few individuals know WHY they do what they do.

To the contrary, Sinek said that effective companies and organizations work from the inside out. The majority of their constituents not only know WHAT they do and HOW they do it, but most importantly, they know WHY they exist. They know WHY they exist because these businesses and organizations start with why. They thoroughly and repeatedly communicate their why. They keep their why crystal clear and in focus. They defend their why because it defines who they are. As a result, they do not worry about the competition. They act differently than their competition because they are different. They think, breathe and live out their why. Moreover, these organizations have increasing numbers of people buying into their why and not their what. People are drawn to why companies and organizations exit.

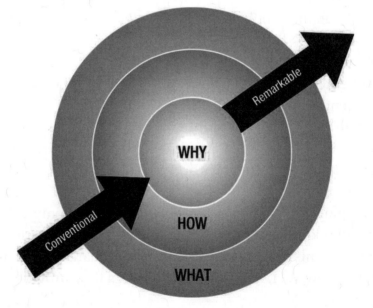

49

Citing a prime example to support his theory, Sinek wrote extensively about the global success of Apple. In recent years, Apple has continued to capture increasing market share; not because people are merely attracted to WHAT they produce, so much as they are inspired and intrigued by their WHY. Where most technology companies start from the outside the Golden Circle and know WHAT products they make, Apple has become an overnight success because they start with WHY they exist. Apple exists to challenge the status quo. Apple created a platform for media called iTunes and it revolutionized the industry; challenging the status quo. Apple created a cell phone that forced carriers to develop an entirely new platform for cell phones, and AT&T was the only willing entrepreneur at the time to accept the challenge. Apple exists to think outside the box, impacting the world through technology. HOW does Apple fulfill their WHY? The company develops innovative, attractive, user-friendly products. WHAT are those products? The list includes iPhones, iPads, iPods, iTunes, computers and a host of additional products with more yet to come. They think and operate from the inside out, asking and knowing WHY they exist.

The exiting and incoming leaders—along with the Elders and executive leadership staff—must start with the WHY of the local church's existence. They must know and accept their God-given mission to seek and to save the lost, then maturing them into fully devoted followers of Christ. Their vision must never become fuzzy or forgotten. Case in point, Sinek cites what has happened with Wal-Mart.

"On April 5, 1992, at approximately eight in the morning, Wal-Mart lost its WHY. On that day, Sam Walton, Wal-Mart's inspired leader, the man who embodied the cause around which he built the world's largest retailer, died in the University of Arkansas Medical Science Hospital in Little Rock of bone marrow cancer. Soon after, Walton's oldest son, S. Robeson Walton, who succeeded his father as chairman of the company, gave a public statement. 'No changes are expected in the corporate direction, control or policy,' he said. Sadly for Wal-Mart employees, customers and shareholders, that is not what happened."[28]

When Walton founded Wal-Mart, he did so on a WHY that was focused on people. He showed up to work on Saturdays because his people had to work on Saturday. He drove his dogs around in the back of his old pick-up truck, wearing a trucker's cap and an old tweed jacket. He stayed faithful to his roots and he connected with those he sought to serve; the common, average American. It is no wonder that under his leadership, Wal-Mart captured the attention of America. People flocked to his stores because they were attracted to his WHY.

But following his death, Wal-Mart's WHY became both fuzzy and forgotten. It morphed from people to profit. Wal-Mart's public image became tainted, particularly in light of the many lawsuits filed against the business by their own employees. One CEO after another has taken the company

---

[28] Simon Sinek. *Start With Why: How Great Leaders Inspire Everyone to Take Action* (New York: The Penguin Group, 2009), p. 202.

51

further from their original WHY, and should the company attempt to recast their original vision, the CEO must embrace the WHY of the company in the way that he acts. Case in point: while he led the company, Sam Walton never received a salary higher than $350,000, as compared to the multimillion pay packages of his successors.[29]

If we are to experience an effective leader><shift; we must know, accept, protect and pay the high cost of the mission—the WHY—of the local church. As one leader leaves, another must arrive to pursue the WHY, not the WHAT. If the incoming leader doesn't understand or grasp the WHY, an ineffective—and potentially catastrophic—transition may happen. Moreover, this demands that the current leadership have a clear and unmistakable vision as to WHY they exist.

In 1983, Steve Jobs lured John Sculley away from Pepsi to serve as the president of Apple. Sculley led Pepsi to remarkable levels of achievement, becoming a serious competitor to the soft drink giant, Coca-Cola. Sculley was a known business genius, but he was not a visionary. After a short two years, Steve Jobs did not see eye-to-eye with Sculley or Apple's board of directors and he resigned—but he came back in 1997 to run the company because Jobs believed in the WHY. Something similar happened when Michael Dell resigned as the CEO of Dell Corporation, only to return a few years later. The same happened at Starbucks when Howard Schultz resigned as CEO in 2000, only to return in 2008. In these instances, successors—though they are gifted and highly skilled business professionals—they did not inspire people

---

[29] Ibid., pp. 202-206.

with the WHY of their companies. As a result, their companies began to falter and stall.[30]

When a leader><shift takes place within the church, the incoming leader must live, eat and breathe the vision, the mission, the WHY of the church. If not, the succession will not succeed. The retired leader just might have to reappear on center stage to recast the vision, as did returning CEOs of companies. Gifted, high capacity leaders are able to inspire people to take action in advancing the kingdom of God—not in advancing themselves. People are drawn to the WHY of a mission-driven church and not the WHAT of a program-driven church.

It was a summer day in 1963 and over a quarter of a million people stood at the steps of the Abraham Lincoln Memorial in our nation's capital. The speaker that day was Dr. Martin Luther King, and he delivered a speech that has become one of the most widely known and remembered by people throughout this modern era. With a booming voice, King declared, "I have a dream..." He did not say, "I have a program, I have a plan, etc." He cast a vision for America, and people embraced it. People came out for a cause that day, and not for a speech. That moment was catalytic, inspiring millions of people to join the cause for racial equality in our nation. It was all about the WHY. Why did Jesus resolutely set out for Jerusalem? He was on a mission to seek and to save us. He died, was buried, raised from the dead and seated on His throne in heaven. For Jesus, it was 'mission accomplished'.

---

[30] Ibid., pp.193-199.

Push pause.
Will we say the same—'mission accomplished'?
If not, why not?

Part II
The Plan

Reality #5:
A Plan Brings Success to Succession

*"Plans fail for lack of counsel,
but with many advisers they succeed."*
Proverbs 15:22

It was unheard of. No one had yet made the attempt to discover the South Pole, but Norwegian explorer Roald Amundsen (1872-1928) was determined to do so. From 1910-12, Amundsen and his team traveled across the polar icecap at the bottom of the world, and in December, 1911, Roald Amundsen discovered the South Pole. He and his team traveled to a place where no living person had ever been.

One of the secrets to his success was his preparation. Long before he set off in search of the South Pole, he set off for Spain. Traveling from his home in Norway, the twenty-something Amundsen journeyed nearly two-thousand miles to Spain—by bicycle. It was the year 1899—more than a decade before he would set off on his polar expedition. Moreover, Amundsen thought through every element of what he would someday face in Antarctica, and he prepared for it. He lived for a time with Eskimos, learning from them how to survive in extreme polar conditions. He learned to dress in heavy, loose fitting clothing like them; train and use dog sleds as did they; and even to develop a slow and methodical pace similar to theirs. Amundsen even learned to eat raw dolphin meat in the event he would become stranded and have nothing else to eat if he hoped to survive. Looking back on his history making achievement, Amundsen wrote:

> "I may say that this is the greatest factor—the way in which the expedition is equipped—the way in which every difficulty is foreseen, and precautions taken for meeting or avoiding it. Victory awaits him who has everything in order — luck, people call it. Defeat is certain for him who has neglected to take the necessary precautions in time; this is called bad luck."[31]

Amundsen may have called it luck, but deep down he knew that his success was due in large part to his preparation. He trained, and then trained some more. He studied, and then studied some more. In order to successfully travel to a land where he had never been, he carefully and deliberately prepared for more than a decade. The men who risked their lives in traveling with him would have been more grateful for Amundsen's exercise of self-leadership. After all, how can one lead others if he cannot lead himself? This very truth is captured in *Great by Choice*.

> "Amundsen's philosophy: You don't wait until you're in an unexpected storm to discover that you need more strength and endurance. You don't wait until you're shipwrecked to determine if you can eat raw dolphin. You don't wait until you're on the Antarctic journey to become a superb skier and dog handler. You prepare

---

[31] Roald Amundsen, *The South Pole: An Account of the Norwegian Antarctic Expedition in the "Fram," 1910–1912*, (translated by A. G. Chater, 1912).

with intensity, all the time, so that when conditions turn against you, you can draw from a deep reservoir of strength. And equally, you prepare so that when conditions turn in your favor, you can strike hard."[32]

Push pause.
Can the same be said of us? Like Amundsen, are we practicing self-leadership by preparing to go to a place we've not been? Are we able to lead others in our care because we have done our due diligence by preparing to transition away from the church? How are you preparing to take your team to where you have not yet been? Based on your preparation, is your team willing to follow you to a place of transition?

A FAILURE TO PLAN IS PLANNING TO FAIL

A leader><shift can and will take us to a land of post-ministry. To experience success in the time of succession, we must prepare for every contingency, just as did Amundsen. He was responsible for the physical well-being of men in his care, and we are responsible for the spiritual well-being of people in our care.

In these next four chapters, we explore the importance of developing a plan for succession. Remember that each local church is a living entity, and just as there are no two people who are exactly alike, the same is true of the church—there are no two exactly alike. Every congregation has its own unique

---

[32] Jim Collins and Morten T. Hansen. *Great by Choice* (New York: HarperBusiness, 2011), pp. 14-15.

spiritual DNA, making it necessary for each church to develop its own unique succession plan. What works in one church will not necessarily work in another. To that end, the exiting pastor and the elder team must work together to develop their succession plan. The pastor cannot develop the plan alone, nor should the Elders develop the plan without the insight and involvement of the exiting pastor. Proverbs 15:22 states, "Plans fail for lack of counsel, but with many advisers they succeed."

There is greater likelihood of putting success in succession when we work synergistically together. On September 12, 1962, while speaking at Rice University, then-president John F. Kennedy made a startling announcement that many of us can recall verbatim: "We choose to go to the moon. We choose to go to the moon in this decade, not because it is easy, but because it is hard." Moreover, his declaration was later fulfilled before the end of the decade, when on July 20, 1969, the late Neil Armstrong was the first person to step foot on the moon. That historic achievement was made possible by a group of people developing a plan. Armstrong could not have accomplished that mission through his own planning. What one person could not do, a team of individuals did together. We cannot accomplish effective leader><shifts without a team of people working together to develop a succession plan.

It is an age old fact that when we fail to plan, we plan to fail—and the failure can impact the local church over the long term. Not all ineffective leader><shifts are as catastrophic as what happened to the Crystal Cathedral, but more commonly, the local church experiences lost opportunities and momentum when there is no pre-determined succession plan.

Case in point; consider what happened in these recent years to "First Christian Church," a real congregation but with a fictitious name for the purpose of telling their story. While interviewing a number of people for this study, the executive pastor and an elder of the church indicated to me that the long-term, endeared pastor of the megachurch refused to discuss the development of a succession plan. Though he was able to lead the church to grow by thousands, the pastor refused to lead well in the end because he refused to talk about his eventual transition.

It should not surprise us then that when the senior pastor finally retired, the church floundered; and not just for a brief period of time, but for years. Many left the church for other congregations, and a rift took place between the leadership and the people who remained in the church. The church spent years finding the pastor's successor, and he stayed only a few years. Then, the church spent another two years looking for another successor, and once he was located, he stayed only a few years. As of this writing, the congregation recently hired the third minister to follow the beloved pastor. The executive minister said that the impact of having no succession plan was negatively felt more than fifteen years into the future. He indicated that the church lost tremendous momentum because they spent more than five years looking for successors, during which time the church had no central voice to cast vision, and growing apprehension between the congregation and the Elders created an environment of distrust. The loss of momentum could have been avoided had the exiting senior minister developed a succession plan. Succession planning is essential; it is not negotiable.

60

WHY SUCCESSION PLANNING IS NECESSARY

Bob Russell, in his book *Transition Plan*, provides a number of personal insights on transitions after completing an effective leader><shift at Southeast Christian Church in Louisville, Kentucky. Regarding an actual succession plan, Russell states: "God can bless a variety of transitions, but an intentional plan has the best chance of success. For every church that has experienced a smooth transition with no transition plan, there are five that really struggled."[33]

Under Bob Russell's leadership, Southeast Christian Church became one of America's largest churches, and he knew that as a matter of stewardship, there had to be an effective transition between himself and his successor, Dave Stone. To that end, the Elders and Russell developed an intentional succession plan, believing that such a plan would provide the church with a smooth and effective transition. Even though leaders in other congregations are not of this opinion, Russell and the elder team believed it to be logical and right.

> "Some ministers feel the choice of their successor should be left up to God and that any effort at a transition plan is a presumption on God's will. But we don't take that same approach to other transitions. We make out a will for our children, we train someone to take our place at work, and we mentor assistant coaches in athletics. Why should we give less attention to the kingdom of God?"[34]

---

[33] Bob Russell and Bryan Bucher. *Transition Plan* (Louisville, KY: Ministers Label Publishing, 2010). pp. 57-58.
[34] Ibid., p. 18.

Russell urges his colleagues to give serious thought to the need for a succession plan, citing five practical reasons for coming to grips with this season of life. First, he reminds us that there is a cycle to life and that we are going to die. If that reason does nothing to move us to give thought to succession, perhaps his second reason will. Russell reminds us that we lose energy and imagination as we age. We find it difficult to adapt to change. Then thirdly, as a natural result of not remaining relevant, aging ministers lose the ability to inspire the next generation. Fourth, we should give thought to transition because we are entering into a new season of life that can breathe life into us. There is life after ministry. We just need to make certain that we are developing a post-pastorate identity, which is discussed in part four of this book. Finally, Russell reminds us that if we are to be exceptional leaders, we must put the welfare of the local church ahead of our own. Whatever it takes, be certain as leaders to lead the charge in developing an intentional plan of succession.[35]

Intentional planning is a biblical principle. Throughout Scripture, we find rich evidence of managerial planning. For example, in Genesis 41, Joseph was appointed second-in-command of Egypt to develop a plan that would save that nation—and surrounding nations—from certain starvation. During seven years of record harvest, a team of people built granaries in which to store excess grain that would later feed millions of people during seven years of record famine. Joseph executed a plan. Nehemiah serves as another example. After he examined the debris field around the city of Jerusalem,

---

[35] Ibid., pp. 42-45.

Nehemiah and his team developed a plan to rebuild the city walls in a record fifty-two days. Even Jesus instructed His disciples to follow a plan to reach others with the Good News; and that by first being His witnesses in Jerusalem, then in Judea, followed by Samaria, and then to the ends of the earth. Because the disciples followed a deliberate and intentional plan, the world continues to learn about Jesus Christ. What would have happened in all of these examples if there were no plans? Planning is not being sinful, it is being responsible. Moreover, when a team of people take part in developing and executing a plan, the individuals involved are highly valued, leading to a greater degree of succes

Following Roald Amundsen's discovery of the South Pole in 1911, a number of polar expeditions were launched. One of the most renowned polar explorers was Earnest Shackleton, who led an expedition to Antarctica in 1914. His ship, the *Endurance*, was trapped in an ice pack and eventually crushed. In extreme cold, the food shortages and the loss of their ship created great anxiety to the crew. Yet, Shackleton and his crew survived. Their plan to survive worked. Inspired by the servant leadership of Shackleton, the crew shared their dwindling food rations with one another, and they risked their lives for one another. Shackleton even gave away his mittens and boots to others, while serving during the longest watches of the night. Eventually, the entire crew of the *Endurance* was saved. Not a single life was lost.

Regretfully, the same cannot be said about the polar explorer Vilhjalmur Stefansson, who led a Canadian expedition to the North Pole. Like the *Endurance*, Stefansson's ship the *Karluk* became trapped in the polar ice pack and was eventually crushed. Unlike Shackleton, Stefansson was driven by the objective to reach the North Pole at all costs. Everything else was secondary to this one goal, even the survival of his crew. Facing starvation in the vast artic region, Stefansson's crew turned on one another, and to no one's surprise, every crew member died—including Stefansson. In their thinking, it was every man for himself. All eleven lives were lost.[36]

When approaching the autumn years of ministry, we must lead with a servant's heart. It is essential that we put the needs of the body of Christ before our own needs. Moreover, we must invite others to join us in developing a succession plan. By doing so, not only will we end up with a far more effective transition, but we will also invest value in the lives of others with whom we lead. There is no substitute for this step in handing off the baton of leadership to the next generation. As well, there is no excuse for not getting this essential aspect of succession planning accomplished. The Word clearly states: "Plans fail for lack of counsel, but with many advisers they succeed."[37]

Push pause.

If you have not discussed a succession plan for your transition with other leaders, when do you plan to do so? What are necessary components of a succession plan for your location of ministry? Who do you need to invite into the discussion of your succession planning?

---

[36] Dennis N.T. Perkins, *Leading at the Edge* (New York: AMACOM, 2000), pp. xiii-xiv.
[37] Proverbs 15:22.

Reality #6:
A New Plan for a New Day

"Brothers and sisters, choose seven men from among you
who are known to be full of the Spirit and wisdom.
We will turn this responsibility over to them
and will give our attention to prayer and the ministry of the word."
Acts 6:3-4

It had not happened for six hundred years. Around the world, Roman Catholics were stunned at the decision of then-Pope Benedict to resign his pontificate while still alive. For six centuries, there was only one succession plan in the papacy. The outgoing pope left office on the day he died. At the age of eighty-five and while in declining health, Benedict realized that he was no longer physically able to lead the Catholic Church. After all, leadership has a shelf life.

With courage and determination, Benedict did what the world least expected. He willingly became less and allowed someone else to become more. On February 28, 2013, then-Pope Benedict instituted a new succession plan because, in his thinking, the old plan would not work in this new day. While becoming increasingly frail as he aged, Benedict knew that staying any longer in the papacy would only hurt the Catholic Church and not help.

Our culture doesn't think this way. Whether on the job, in a friendship, or pursuing a project; we are driven to the next achievement. We strive to achieve more, earn more, and have more; but not Benedict XVI. Acting in a counter cultural way, the former pope stepped away from the most powerful position in the Roman Catholic world so that he could experience life in a more common way. The BBC reported that the pope emeritus spoke from a window in his new residence in Castel Gandolfo and said, "I will simply be a pilgrim who is starting the last phase of his pilgrimage on this earth."[38]   With the world watching, the College of Cardinals declared that it was 'out with the old and in with the new' when it came to the papal succession plan.

A NEW PLAN FOR A NEW DAY

In Acts 6:1-7, Luke described for us a moment in the early church when a new plan had to be developed. The church was growing by the thousands, and the apostles were struggling with leading and serving effectively. Case in point, the Greek speaking widows were overlooked in the daily distribution of food. This oversight caused conflict within the church and needed to be resolved, so the apostles analyzed the situation and formulated a new and appropriate plan. Men who were known to be full of both wisdom and the Holy Spirit were chosen to distribute food to the widows, so that the apostles could focus their efforts on prayer and the teaching of Scripture.   When they implemented the new plan; disadvantaged widows were fed, unity was restored and the church flourished with many more thousands of people coming to faith in Christ. It was 'out with the old and in with the new.' A new day called for a new plan.

The same is true of the church today. Far too many churches are defaulting to old and dated methods of

---

[38] http://www.bbc.co.uk/news/world-europe-21624149

succession. Church growth authority Dr. Lyle Schaller lectures on this very issue. The Virginia Baptist Mission Board invited Schaller to speak to the leaders of eight large congregations on the topic of succession planning. Held in Chicago, the conference featured Schaller giving timely advice for "making a smooth transition," as articulated in the power point presentation still available on the internet.[39] Schaller contends that "the larger the church, the longer the tenure, and the sharper the growth pattern, the more crucial is succession and the more difficult it is to work it out."[40]

To that end, he was explicit in his presentation that there is an old way that no longer works and he suggested a new approach to succession planning. In the past, when a long tenured pastor retired, he was replaced with an interim pastor who served while the church searched for his permanent successor. Once the new pastor accepted the call and relocated, the retired pastor often stayed in the area—and sometimes in the same church as pastor emeritus. In this old model, a pulpit committee typically locates the new pastor using limited tools and methods to complete the search. All too often, the successor pastor is not a match for the church culture and does not relate well to the congregation or community. Moreover, relational conflicts often result between the incoming and the retiring pastors because they did not have the opportunity to work with one another on the church staff.

---

[39]http://www.google.com/url?sa=t&rct=j&q=&esrc=s&frm=1&source=web&cd=1&ved=0CCsQFjAA&url=http%3A%2F%2Fwww.vbmb.org%2FServices%2FStaff-Transitions%2Fmedia%2Fdocs%2FBonsack-Succession.ppt&ei=HBfiUcWxA4i2yAHlmoHgCg&usg=AFQjCNEG87pHITMuWvoDHXoCZF_8QKiTNg&sig2=KXfl7XGibdUBBtoy2q31DA

[40] Ibid.

Schaller believes that a new, more appropriate plan is needed to bring about a smooth transition. Succession planning is not limited to just finding a new pastor. Schaller suggests that the retiring pastor form a small team comprised of both staff and lay leaders to create a strategic plan for the immediate and intermediate future of the congregation. Once the strategic plan is formulated, Schaller recommends that the same team then determine what kind of a leader (and staff) is needed to pursue and accomplish the strategic plan. He believes that it will take two to three years to locate the new pastor, and the retiring pastor must be heavily involved in the search process. Schaller contends that the church must draw on the knowledge and experience of their long tenured pastor while he is still on staff so that he can help assimilate the new pastor in his leadership role of senior minister.[41] Lyle Schaller is spot on, hitting the nail on the head. There is a desperate need for the local church to develop a new and effective succession plan, while steering clear of old, dated plans from the past.

Push pause.
What transition plans have been used in the past where you serve? What do your governing documents require in terms of finding your successor? Do the requirements look like an older model or method? Like Benedict XVI, how will you initiate a new plan for a new day when it comes to your succession?

---

[41] Ibid.

THINK ANALYTICALLY

Still, another change must take place in our thinking. Americans are well accustomed to a 'one size fits all' mentality. For decades, we have been using this phrase in our speech, but it has also become a welcome part of our lives. From clothing to sports equipment to jewelry and even to military equipment, products are made to fit all sizes of people. Why? It is easy and convenient. It takes little or no effort to make a purchase of an item that fits any individual's given size. A 'one size fits all' mentality has slowly crept into the minds of many church leaders. They think that 'one plan fits all' when it comes to transitions. Whether they consider old and dated plans from the past, or duplicating the succession plan of another church, they think 'one plan fits all,' and they find this approach both easy and convenient. That line of thinking needs to go out the window.

To lead effectively, we must develop and practice the skill of analytical thinking, a skill that is readily identifiable in Scripture. Consider Nehemiah. When he returned to Jerusalem to rebuild the city walls, he examined the debris field at night. That is most interesting. Why at night? Why not during the day when the sun would be bright and he would be able to see clearly? Simply put, Nehemiah wanted to be left alone—to think analytically. When the sun went down, people went into their homes, clearing the streets and closing their shops. People went to bed at night. So, Nehemiah would have been left alone to think strategically, seeing what he was up against in the rebuilding of the walls (see Nehemiah 2:11-18).

Moses sent the spies into Canaan to see what they were facing (see Numbers 13:1-25). The spies were to examine the land; its topography and agriculture. They were to study the people sociologically. For forty days, they were to make observations about the land they were soon to enter. They had to use their minds, thinking analytically and strategically. Not only are there examples of leaders practicing the discipline of analytical thinking, but there is an expectation of Jesus for us to use our minds. Notice what is similar about each of the following verses:

> When Peter came into the house, Jesus was the first to speak. "What do you think, Simon?" he asked. "From whom do the kings of the earth collect duty and taxes— from their own sons or from others?" (Matthew 17:25)

> "What do you think? If a man owns a hundred sheep, and one of them wanders away, will he not leave the ninety-nine on the hills and go to look for the one that wandered off? (Matthew 18:12)

> "What do you think? There was a man who had two sons. He went to the first and said, 'Son, go and work today in the vineyard.'" (Matthew 21:28)

> "What do you think about the Christ? Whose son is he?" (Matthew 22:42)

Do you hear and see the recurring question? Four times, Jesus posed the question, "What do you think?" There is a rule in hermeneutics (i.e., the science of biblical interpretation) that when something is repeated, it is important. When something

70

repeats in the text, God attempts to get our attention with that particular word or phrase. So, in this instance, when Jesus repeatedly asked, "What do you think," He infers that we are to use our minds. Jesus wants us to think.

In 1 Chronicles 12:32, we read that "the sons of Issachar were men who had minds to understand the times and they knew what Israel should do." The context of this verse is full of insight. King Saul was no longer leading Israel. He had committed suicide in battle, and David was now king. The nation of Israel was at a defining moment, and there were men who were skilled at reading—or analyzing—their culture and they knew how to respond as a nation. In the same manner, we must develop and practice the skill of analytical thinking, particularly when a succession is on the horizon. The leaders of the church must work together in developing a specific plan that is unique to the local church, and that can only be done by taking the time to pray, talk and think.

ASK 'WHERE ARE WE' AND 'WHERE ARE WE HEADED'

To develop an effective succession plan for the future, leaders need to determine where the church is in the present. Every church has a life cycle, and it is essential for leaders to know where they are at the present if they hope to be able to lead the church to a healthy place in the future following a leader><shift. Geoff Surratt, the managing director of Exponential, lectures on the life cycle of a church, saying that churches tend to grow for fifteen years and then they level off. After fifteen years, a church will 1) plateau, or 2) decline, or 3) catch a new wave of innovation and begin to grow again. When the church plateaus, leaders throw money at a number of

71

initiatives, trying to restart numerical growth. They build a new addition—or an entirely new building. They relocate or launch a satellite location. They hire staff. Leaders expect churches to continually grow, yet even the churches that the Apostle Paul planted no longer exist.[42]

Just as a person passes through various stages of a life cycle, the same can be said of the church. A congregation starts by being birthed and then enters the childhood stage. A "child church" is concerned primarily with survival, asking: "Do we get to do this again next week? How many people were here this weekend, and how much was the offering?" The next stage is the adult stage, followed by the parent stage. When the local church is in either of these stages, their goal is to reproduce spiritually, though the majority of churches in America are not doing so. The next stage of church life is long sought after, and it is the grandparent stage; when the local church has the ability to share generously with others, particularly with the next generation. Finally, the life cycle of a church ends with the Senior Citizen stage, when the goal is to leave behind a strong legacy.

Think carefully on this. A person can be in multiple stages at the same time: a person can be an adult, parent and grandparent all at the same time. The same can be said of the local church. A church can be well established into the adult season of its life cycle, while also experiencing the parent and grandparent seasons of its spiritual journey. When formulating a succession plan for the church, leaders must determine where the church is in its life cycle. Why? Each stage of the life cycle

---

[42] Geoff. Dallas Surrat, Texas: Leadership Network Pastor-to-Pastor Mentoring Seminar; May 2, 2013.

has its own unique focus of attention. For example, if the church is in the Grandparent and Senior Citizen stages, leaders must determine what kind of spiritual fruit they are bearing. They should determine if the church is an orchard. A modern day parable would sound like this. Is the church like a man pouring his entire life into his one and only apple tree? Over the years, it produces apples. He travels in every direction, telling people about how to grow an apple tree. Eventually, his apple tree produces fewer apples and eventually stops bearing fruit at all. No longer is the guy asked to come and speak about how to grow an apple tree, and he is left sitting beside a dying apple tree. On the other hand, while in the Grandparent and Senior Citizen stage, is the church more like a man who is determined to keep planting more and more apple trees, while teaching others to do the same? Is the church willing to send him to the many places asking him to come and equip others to do the same?

When formulating a succession plan, it is of vital importance to answer these two questions: at what life stage is the local church and what is its focus? Perhaps the beloved, long tenured pastor is sitting beside an apple tree that is dying. The local church he leads has born little or no spiritual fruit in years. The succession plan must then address the issue of immediacy in finding a visionary pastor with the energy and will to revitalize the local church. If, on the other hand, the long tenured pastor is leading a vibrant, growing church at the time of his transition, the succession plan will look very different in terms of who is called and when the transition actually happens. Think analytically. One plan does not fit all.

One of the most effective leaders in the early church was the Apostle Paul. While imprisoned, Paul wrote a moving letter to the Church in Philippi, and in the letter, Paul made a strong statement: "But one thing I do: Forgetting what is behind and straining toward what is ahead, I press on toward the goal to win the prize for which God has called me heavenward in Christ Jesus. All of us who are mature should take such a view of things" (Phil. 3:13-15). Paul did not live in the past. He did not dwell on his many previous accomplishments, nor was he consumed with the problems he faced in the present. Paul made it a practice to be forward thinking. He thought about life in eternity with Christ. He thought about the tomorrows of life. Moreover, Paul said that those who are spiritually mature should take such a view of things.

Leaders in the church are assumed to be spiritually mature, and being mature, they should be forward in their thinking, as was Paul. Though we learn from the past, we do not live there; and as a result, leaders need to be thinking analytically as to how to move the church forward, advancing the kingdom of God. When we formulate a succession plan, we want it to move the local church forward. We do not want to lose momentum when we lose a long tenured pastor. After all, leaders lead by moving people forward.

To that end, prior to the development of a succession plan, leaders should have the vision, mission and core values of the church firmly in place and functioning. The vision—or the dream they want to come true—provides momentum for the church, particularly when making a senior pastor transition. If the vision, mission and core values have not been developed, it is essential that leaders analytically think through these issues

74

prior to developing a succession plan. How can we call a new pastor to a church when we do not know who we are and where we are going as a church? Moreover, if a church has an established and known vision, and they live, eat and breathe the vision, they will want the new pastor to embrace, honor and pursue that same vision. If he doesn't do so, the succession will be far from effective and momentum will be lost. Before duplicating the succession plan of another church, determine God's vision, mission and core values of the church you lead; and only then begin to develop your unique, one-of-a-kind succession plan that fits the spiritual DNA of your church. After all, there is no such thing as one plan fits all.

The founding leaders of Australia desired to move people forward. They even communicated that desire through the coat of arms they developed in the early years of their nation. It depicts two creatures that are indigenous to Australia: the kangaroo and the emu. These two creatures share a common trait; they cannot move backwards. An emu is a flightless bird with three-toed feet, and as a result, it can only move forward. Likewise, a kangaroo's tail prevents it from moving in a backward direction. Both creatures can only move forward, and the Australian coat of arms declares that same intent that as a nation, they will only move forward. The Church must move forward, and moving the Church forward is the responsibility of the leadership thinking analytically, particularly when a leader><shift is about to take place.

Nobel Prize winning economist and psychologist Daniel Kahneman challenges us to think more slowly because we do not think correctly. He has become a recognized authority on how well we think. In an interview with *Time* magazine, Kahneman commented about our inability to think well.

> "We are normally blind about our own blindness. We're generally overconfident in our opinions and our impressions and judgments. We exaggerate how knowable the world is ....What psychology and behavioral economics have shown is that people don't think very carefully. They're influenced by all sorts of superficial things in their decision-making, and they procrastinate and don't read the small print."[43]

According to Kahneman, we need to realize how poorly we think and chose to think differently. In his book *Thinking, Fast and Slow*, he posed a simple question to illustrate the importance of slowing down and thinking correctly. The puzzle goes like this: "Do not try to solve [this puzzle] but listen to your intuition: A bat and a ball cost $1.10. The bat costs one dollar more than the ball. How much does the ball cost?"[44]

In his book, Kahneman noted that the majority of people give a quick—and wrong—answer; that being ten cents. If we take the time to think through the puzzle more carefully, we would realize that if the ball costs ten cents, the total cost is $1.20 ($1.10 for the bat and 10 cents for the ball). The correct answer—that may take more time to reach—is that the ball costs five cents. Kahneman explained in his book that more

---

[43] Belinda Luscombe, "10 Questions" *Time*, November 28, 2011, p. 104.
[44] Daniel Kahneman, *Thinking, Fast and Slow*. New York: Farrar, Strauss and Giroux; 2011; pp. 44-45.

than half of the students at Princeton, MIT and Harvard reached the wrong answer, and at less prestigious schools, more than eighty percent of the students were wrong. Kahneman urged his readers to think more slowly and with a greater focus and intent because it does not come naturally to us.

When it comes time to formulate a succession plan, one plan does not fit all. We will need to slow down and think analytically about our individual ministry location. We need to focus intently on answering these questions: where are we in the life cycle of a church or ministry and what is our vision? Thinking more deeply will enable us to develop a plan of succession more decisively. After all, deeper thinking—like succession planning—doesn't come naturally to us.

Push pause.
As a ministry, where are we now and where are we headed? What is our vision (i.e., the dream we want to come true)? What is our mission (i.e., how the dream will come true)? What are our rank-ordered core values (i.e., like the internal operating system of a computer)?

Reality #7:
The Plan is About More than a Person

"And now let Pharaoh look for a discerning and wise man and put him in charge of the land of Egypt."
Genesis 41:33

Every year, millions of Americans spend billions of dollars to correct their vision, and I am one of those Americans. For years, I have struggled with myopia, more commonly known as being nearsighted. Since middle school, glasses and contacts have corrected my nearsightedness. But recently, my continuing struggle with myopia was more permanently corrected by laser eye surgery. Tens of millions of Americans struggle with nearsightedness, and they must make a decision to have corrected it or not. Regretfully, leaders of churches and ministries struggle in much the same way when it comes time for a leader><shift.

Leaders of churches and parachurch organizations are near-sighted when transitions are about to happen. Leadership teams are focused primarily on finding the right successor. When the long tenured leader is about to leave, all eyes are on the successor. Being nearsighted at this pivotal moment in the life cycle of the church or ministry organization can lead to a failed transition. Leaders must expand their focus to a number of issues that are intricately involved in succession. Leaders must make a decision to correct their blurred nearsightedness and look beyond just the issue of finding the right person, and they must give focused attention on the many different parts of an effective succession plan. This chapter helps us to think beyond the need to simply find the right successor and to develop a succession plan with a number of helpful parts.

In ancient Egypt, a survival plan—not a succession plan—of many parts was developed. Egypt was facing unprecedented times of plenty and want; seven years of record harvests were to be followed by seven years of record famine. God revealed this to the Pharaoh in two different dreams, and God enabled the young man Joseph to interpret both dreams that had the same meaning. As a result, Joseph was the discerning and wise man who Pharaoh appointed to lead Egypt through fourteen years the likes of which the nation had never before known. Though not described in Scripture, we can confidently assume that Joseph's survival plan had many parts. He would have had to develop planting and harvesting strategies, as well as to build a number of grain storage facilities throughout the entire nation of Egypt. He had to develop accounting systems to measure and calculate grain inventories, as well as to monitor distribution of the grain during the lengthy famine. Just as his survival plan had many parts, so also, our succession plan must have many parts. Moreover, our never changing God can make us to be wise and discerning leaders to develop and execute an effective succession plan.

QUESTIONS NEED ANSWERS

Whether spoken or not, questions arise in the minds of people when an anticipated transition is on the horizon. When it becomes increasingly apparent that a long tenured leader is leaving, people begin asking questions of leaders and one another. Casual conversations begin to steer in the direction of the unknown, and members of the church or ministry organization begin to wonder about the immediate future of their believing community. Like popcorn popping in hot oil, many logical and expected questions pop up from people, such as:

→ Who is the successor?
→ When is our pastor leaving?
→ Where will we find his replacement?
→ Is the new pastor already on our staff or will be hire someone new?
→ Is our pastor staying here after he retires?
→ If he stays, will he be pastor emeritus on our staff?
→ Who is leading this process?
→ Is the pastor involved in finding his replacement?
→ How will the congregation be involved in this process?
→ From what outside voices do we need to hear?
→ How long should the transition take?
→ Will others on the staff stay or will they have to leave?
→ How can we keep God at the center of this change?
→ Will our retiring pastor help our new pastor in making the transition?

The list of questions goes on and on, and if questions are not answered by the leadership, people will come up with their own answers and the answers are often wrong. A succession plan, which is made up of many parts, can help answer questions that are on the minds of people. Though the following are suggested parts of a succession plan, every church or ministry organization must develop a plan unique to their situation. For example, if a church has not funded the retirement of their long tenured pastor, their plan must thoroughly address retirement income; whereas if a church has provided their retiring pastor with a sufficient pension, this part of the succession plan is of less concern.

Keep in mind that we are speaking of a succession plan to be followed when a long tenured pastor retires, which we can refer to as 'Plan B.' Whereas 'Plan A' is commonly referred to as the 'getting hit by a bus plan.' Every church and parachurch organization needs a Plan A in place should there be an unexpected and untimely exit of the primary leader. His exit may be due to illness, injury, death, or because of a moral lapse. In any event, you must have an actual succession plan in place to maintain the momentum of the organization when a there is a sudden leadership void.

Think with me. Though Apple continues to impact the world with innovative technology, the company still experiences difficulty. In the spring of 2013, **USA Today** reported, "The Apple stock crash is reaching a historic order of magnitude, shaking the faith of investors who piled on in large part on Jobs' showmanship."[45] Investor shares were down forty-four percent, reducing shareholder wealth by $291.2 billion. What caused this massive loss of company value at Apple? Though the article noted that the causes may be complex, the article proposed the death of Steve Jobs on October 5, 2011, Apple's cofounder, as the primary reason.

---

[45] Mark Krantz, "Leadership Loss Shocks Stocks," *USA Today Money*, April 19, 2013.

Organizations have been known to struggle in the absence of an effective leader. The article noted "the fact that a sick or dying CEO is generally a big problem right away for stocks, and when that individual leaves the organization the 'short term shock' evolves into "long term disappointment."[46]

The same is true of the local church or ministry organization. The sudden absence of an effective pastor or parachurch leader can cause more than a hiccup. If the church or ministry carries significant debt, the leader's sudden loss can cause a precipitous drop in giving, which in turn, may cause a negative cash flow. When debt cannot be serviced or payroll funded, the ministry will lose momentum. It is a common and right business practice to carry key man life insurance on the pastor or ministry executive as a financial safeguard. This is an essential consideration for a written Plan A, and with that being said, we now turn our attention to Plan B—the development of a written succession plan.

Push pause.
Do you have a succession "plan A"? If so, where is it written down? Who helped develop this plan and how widely is it known? How have you planned for a continuing income stream following your untimely and premature exit from your ministry?

ESSENTIAL PARTS OF A SUCCESSION PLAN

Though each church and ministry organization is uniquely different, there are certain issues that must be

---

[46] Ibid.

addressed in all ministry related succession plans. These non-negotiable items will be handled in ways distinctive to each organization, and as a result, some issues will be more complex than others. Still, the following items must be a part of your conversation in formulating your actual succession plan, and you may think of still more. The suggestions that follow are to help stir your thinking as a team so that you compile a list of items that will eventually comprise your succession plan. When we buy something that we have to assemble, the box often includes a parts list with the assembly instructions. As leaders, brainstorm a parts list of your succession plan. Moreover, as your leadership team invests time to discuss and develop the succession plan, be sure to put it into writing. Do not leave it partially articulated in cryptic meeting minutes. The succession plan must be a carefully written document that will answer the questions being asked by a myriad of people. A fully and meticulously written succession plan will help the principle people involved in the transition, as well as to reassure people within the believing community. As you read the following, please keep in mind that a number of the following items will be more thoroughly explored in Part 3: The Process and Part 4: The People.

First of all, there are a number of issues involving the retiring pastor, or exiting leader (EL). Of critical importance is the issue of his involvement in the actual transition. As discussed earlier in *Leader>\<Shift*, an effective transition will involve the EL throughout the process. There is an old school of thought that assumes the retiring pastor is to have nothing to do with succession, particularly in choosing his successor. Such thinking is wrong thinking, and has often resulted in poor

decisions being made. Describe in detail how the retiring pastor is to be involved in the succession process. An essential part of this issue is his role in selecting and assisting his successor. Determine what voice the EL will have in the selection of his successor, and how he will be involved in mentoring or helping that individual to transition in his new role.

Careful thought must be given to the actual way in which the retiring pastor becomes less while the successor becomes more, as discussed earlier in *Leader><Shift*. Determine an actual strategy as to how the retiring pastor will preach and teach less often, as well as in having a decreasing voice in meetings while his successor's voice is heard more distinctively. The plan should include a way for the retiring pastor to introduce and transition the successor within groups or ministry teams of influence within the church.

The succession plan must address post-retirement issues for the EL. Again, the old school of thought assumes that a retired pastor must leave and find another church home. This is based on the wrong assumption that he will interfere with his newly appointed successor. Granted, a number of failed successions have happened because of meddling retired pastors who weren't able to hand off the proverbial baton of leadership to the next generation. However, a proper and actual hand off of leadership can happen without the long tenured pastor and his wife having to find a new church home. If we intentionally discuss and develop this part of the succession plan, a win-win can be achieved and all for the glory of God.

Think with me. When I retire and leave The Creek, should I have to find another church to attend? After decades of investing my life here, should I be "homeless" and on the street, having no church home? It does not make sense, and it certainly does not honor God. Leah and I poured our lives into this community, while people poured their lives into ours. Our sons came to faith at The Creek. They grew up here, were married here, and both of our sons were ordained as pastors by the Elders of this congregation. Even some of our grandchildren have been baptized here. For Leah and me, this is home. It does not make sense to put 'grandpa and grandma' out on the street simply because some people assume that I will meddle in my successor's ability to lead in my place.

To help insure a more healthy relationship between the retiring pastor and his successor, put in writing the post-retirement role of the exiting pastor. If he is to remain on staff, describe his responsibilities and carefully determine his title and leadership authority—if he has any. This is a critical issue and leaders must deliberately and thoroughly discuss this matter. If the retiring pastor has no sense of direction or identity outside of his pre-retirement role, provide vocational and spiritual counseling for both the pastor and his wife. Enable them to take a lengthy sabbatical in hopes of developing a sense of direction for serving God in an active retirement. If the retiring pastor remains as an active member in the church he has served, it is important for him to be away from the congregation for a stated period of time. It is increasingly common for the retiring pastor to not attend the church for a year following the weekend he retires, which provides his successor with an ample window of opportunity to adjust to his new leadership role, while the congregation adjusts to their new leader.

Finally, a necessary part of the succession plan involves money. Like it or not, this topic must be addressed, and if leaders possess integrity, they will deliberately discuss and appropriately give honor to where honor is due. If the congregation has not provided a retirement package for their long tenured pastor, the leaders have some serious thinking and calculating to do. Please do not think that receiving a simple love offering will suffice. One retiring minister was told by the Elder chair of his church that they would "take care of him" when he retired, and the pastor trusted his Elders. Though they had never provided him with a pension, they had planned on giving to him a cash gift upon his retirement. The minister grew excited as he anticipated being financially able to retire, yet imagine his surprise when after he preached his final sermon, he was handed a sealed envelope and in it was a check for $25,000—not nearly enough to meet his financial needs for the months and years to come. Likewise, to the other extreme, do not be like the church where the Elders promised the retiring minister to pay him his full salary until he died, causing continuing financial difficulty for the congregation. Think carefully and responsibly about this crucial issue. It must be a specific part of the written succession plan of the church, and if you need professional counsel from outside the leadership team, go after it. Remember, Scripture assures us that many advisors make victory sure (Proverbs 11:14). So, the above items are mentioned to help stir your thinking, developing a viable and expanded "parts list" for the draft copy of your succession plan.

Push pause.

If you are a part of the leadership team and the long tenured leader is soon to leave, to what degree have you discussed these issues with him? Have you been candid about his post-retirement income? How have you helped him develop a post-retirement plan for continuing to serve God? To what degree have you involved him in helping to find his successor?

Not only are there necessary issues involving the retiring pastor or exiting leader (EL) in a succession plan, but the same can be said of the successor or incoming leader (IL). First and foremost, the leaders must determine what they are looking for in a successor. Like late-night television sensation David Letterman, determine a 'top-ten list' of the most important criteria when looking for a candidate. For example, ten possible non-negotiables could include:

1) Spiritual formation (holiness, humility, prayer, Scripture devotion)
2) Formal education and ministry experience
3) Having compassion for broken, disadvantaged and unbelieving people
4) Gifted in communicating Scripture
5) Possessing leadership skills
6) Being transparent and approachable
7) Enjoying people
8) Having a good work ethic

9) Pursuing life-long learning
10) An authentic call to pastoral ministry

These are merely suggested criteria, and each individual church or parachurch organization must determine what they are looking for in a candidate who will best serve in their given circumstances. Again, just as one size or plan does not fit all, one candidate does not fit all. Take all the time that is necessary to establish the criteria by which a successor will be found.

An essential part of the succession plan for the incoming leader will be a litany of questions to establish that individual's doctrinal beliefs, ministry philosophies, managerial and leadership methods, etc. The leadership team needs to develop a tool by which these vital concerns will be thoroughly explored with the candidate. This litmus test can be a questionnaire that is given to the incoming leader to complete, and is then reviewed by a leadership team charged with the selection of the successor. Personality inventories should be completed. Interviews can then follow, during which time the questionnaire is thoroughly discussed. This aspect must be a part of the written succession plan.

As well, be certain to discuss the age factor. Each church must determine the ideal age of the successor, particularly in light of the people they are trying to reach for Christ. Leaders must remember that the primary mission of the church is to reach people who are not yet believers and Christ-followers. To that end, leaders must study and know their demographics (i.e., what traits describe the community where the church is located, in at least a five mile radius of the main campus). Such information enables the leaders to know the largest age group of people yet to reach, and how that impacts the ideal age for the successor. Moreover, the leadership team needs to determine an appropriate age of the candidate that matches the size and nature of the ministry. Case in point, a successor pastor in his late twenties may not be capable or ready to lead a megachurch numbering a few thousand. Typically, a pastor connects relationally with individuals ten years older and younger than himself; yet that ability may not be sufficient in contributing to an effective transition. A successor may have to be considerably younger than the retiring pastor, and the leadership team needs to determine an ideal age span for the candidate, including it as a part of the succession plan.

Another issue to be discussed involves the existing staff. When a leader><shift takes place, the staff becomes anxious for a number of reasons, and their chief concern is job security. The leadership team needs to discuss to what degree the incoming leader can select the team that will serve beside him. Will he have the authority to "clean house," dismissing anyone and everyone in order to bring on board his own team? This is a critical issue that must be carefully considered because the transition must be as seamless as possible in order to maintain ministry momentum. Granted, a church or ministry organization may be dysfunctional and in need of staffing changes. If that is the case, the leadership team should make note in the written succession plan that it will be the responsibility of the incoming leader to make staffing assessments and changes, if needed. Moreover, it is commonly known that at any one time, ten percent of a church staff is thinking about leaving, and the percentage is considerably higher during times of succession. It is wise for the leadership team to give staff members the

permission to consider leaving on a positive note and with a reasonable severance package. After all, when a long tenured pastor retires, the entire staff team enters a season of transition that can be unsettling for many. Discussing and determining the degree to which to a new leader is permitted to develop his staff is a matter worth writing into the succession plan. These are but a few of the items referencing the incoming leader that must make the 'parts list' and eventual succession plan. More issues concerning the incoming leader are discussed in Part 4: The People.

Push pause.
If you are a part of the leadership team and you are responsible for an effective leader><shift, how have you assessed the kind of an incoming leader that is needed? What traits should he possess? What is his ideal age and background? To what degree have you described this in the written succession plan? Have you considered the impact this transition will have on the remaining staff and to what degree? How have you prepared for staff turnover or necessary endings?

JUST DO IT

Athletic gear giant Nike challenges people to "just do it;" to get up and to get physically active. Like Nike, we need to challenge one another to "just do it" by developing a written succession plan.

A few years ago, a group of us decided to climb the highest free-standing mountain in the world. The "roof of Africa," Mt. Kilimanjaro, stands at 19,341 feet. We had climbed a number of high peaks together, but we had not attempted one that was in extreme altitude. On average, ten people die annually of cerebral or pulmonary edema while attempting to summit Kili. Though the climb was not technical, it was demanding and we had to physically train for the forty-five mile hike. We developed a fitness program and often asked one another what progress we were making in our training program. Moreover, we knew that while climbing Kilimanjaro, we would move through every climate zone on earth—from tropical jungle to polar ice cap. So, we had to determine what gear to take for such a wide variation of temperature and weather. Our trek demanded that we plan ahead. We did not wake up one morning and say to one another, "Let's fly to Tanzania today and climb Kilimanjaro." Our trek required months of deliberate, intentional preparation.

In the same way, the church or ministry organization must deliberately prepare for an arduous trek that will take place at some point in the future. We do not wake up and assume that we can instantly and effectively execute a leader><shift. It will require a carefully and thoughtfully developed written plan of succession. Few churches and ministry organizations are taking the time to prepare for this most certain moment that may be in their not so distant future. Like the many people who start out climbing Kilimanjaro and turn back before reaching the summit, there will be a number of churches and ministries who fail in making an effective leadership transition. That failure will be due largely in part to

their failure to plan. Failing to plan is planning to fail. Have the hard conversation with your colleagues. Talk about the proverbial elephant in the middle of the room. Bring up succession over and over again like a broken record until action is finally taken to develop a written succession plan. Just do it.

Reality #8:
A Team Produces the Plan

"Two are better than one because they have a good return for their labor. If either of them falls down, one can help the other up. But pity anyone who falls and has no one to help them up. Also, if two lie down together, they will keep warm. But how can one keep warm alone. Though one may be overpowered, two can defend themselves. A cord of three strands is not quickly broken."
Ecclesiastes 4:9-12

The "Ikea effect" appears to be real according to a team of researchers from three prestigious universities. The name of their research thesis stems from the love of millions of people worldwide for Ikea, a highly successful retailer based in Sweden. Many products purchased at Ikea require some amount of assembly, and research studies indicated that consumers who assembled their purchases from Ikea held those products in a higher place of value, even though in the end, the product may not have been perfectly put together. The purchaser remains proud of his or her creation, which is the idea behind the "Ikea effect."[47]

As leaders, we must realize that when it comes to a succession plan, some assembly is required – and once completed, it should produce for us the "priesthood of all believers effect." We are told by the Apostle Peter that we

---

[47] http://www.hbs.edu/faculty/Publication%20Files/11-091.pdf

belong to the priesthood of all believers (1 Peter 2:9), and as such, we must work together when it comes to succession planning. There is a principle that "two are better than one," meaning that we cannot go it alone; whether generally through life or spiritually in our walk with God. When it comes to developing a succession plan, it is essential to do so as a team of leaders. If one person tries to accomplish the required assembly, that individual will be frustrated with the end product. Working in a vacuum, he will easily overlook succession details that other individuals could remember to include.

THE ASSEMBLY TEAM

In their book *Planning Your Succession: Preparing for Your Future*, Samuel Chand and Dale Bronner compare successful succession planning to a successful play on the baseball field, executed by three players...

> "That's because the champions on any field never achieve success alone. Actual 'wins' always require a team mindset, a practiced pursuit, and an absence of preoccupation with who 'looks best' or who 'gets the credit.'"[48]

Chand and Bronner know that succession planning is a critical issue for business world, as well as for the church. Their research discovered that forty-six percent of companies with over 1,000 employees had no succession plan in place.

---

[48] Samuel Chand and Dale Bronner. *Planning Your Succession: Preparing for Your Future.* (Highland Park, IL: Mall Publishing, 2008), p. xvi.

They also noted that even though fifty-eight percent of small business owners believe that succession planning is their greatest threat, only thirty-percent of family-owned businesses have given little or no thought to succession planning. The authors are of the opinion that with the retirement of tens of millions of baby-boomers over the next two decades, the next generation may not be large or skilled enough to lead in the absence of a long tenured leader. According to Chand and Bronner, succession planning can give birth to an atmosphere of leadership development.

> "When implemented properly, succession planning creates a leadership culture within the organization. A true leadership culture is one that identifies and develops people who are able to function across an organization, who are cross-trained in a variety of responsibilities, and are ready to adapt to a new role with competence and confidence."[49]

Both Chand and Bronner are unique in that they see succession planning as a vitally important part of organizational health. Both men are pastors, and yet more. Samuel Chand served as a college president and chancellor, while Dale Bronner is on the board of directors and is part owner of a multimillion dollar family owned business. These men have deliberately made succession planning a key element for the future health of the organization of which they were part. They have examined the corporate landscape of America

---

[49] Ibid., pp. 4-6.

and identified a number of healthy companies that put great emphasis on succession planning.

> "Many of America's most-admired companies—GE, Bank of America, Johnson & Johnson, McDonald's and others—have already invested much time, energy and money in this key area. Succession planning, they realize, is about building the organization's future. Selecting and developing the right people is the critical linchpin in that process. Against the background of today's graying executive ranks, they understand that advancing an organization's competitive advantage and effectiveness is all about selecting and developing successors."[50]

Now that we know that "some assembly is required" in the development of a succession plan, some obvious questions need to be asked: Who starts the planning process, and when? Who is on the "assembly team"? Who leads the succession planning team? These are pertinent questions, and when left unanswered, a succession plan is left undone. It is essential that someone in leadership to pursue these questions, to intentionally bring them up in conversation, and that someone typically is the exiting leader. Bob Russell, retired pastor of Southeast Christian Church in Louisville, Kentucky, contends in his book *Transition Plan*:

> "The departing leader should be the initiator of the transition plan, and not the organization...The preacher

---

[50] Ibid., p. 51.

needs to be accountable to the Elders or the Church Board. But the plan for a smooth transition must emanate from the preacher and not the Elders or Church Board—otherwise the transition is on precarious ground. It is wise for the preacher to suggest the successor, the strategy, the departure date, and his intention afterward. The Elders may want to introduce possible improvements, but the preacher needs to initiate the discussion and the Church Board needs to respect his wishes. If they can't do that, then they shouldn't pretend it's a transition when it's really a termination."[51]

Russell hit several proverbial nails on the head with his observation. The most likely person to start and drive the process is the exiting leader. By allowing and enabling him to do so, he is buying into the entire process enthusiastically. For example, if the Elders or Church Board initiates and drives the plan, the exiting minister will quickly and likely assume that the church is trying to get rid of him. Regretfully, the actions of the leaders can be misunderstood and wrongly interpreted by the people of the church and not only by the exiting leader. Significant division could result within the church or organization if the exiting leader does not initiate and drive the succession planning process. Moreover, it is important to note that he cannot operate as the "Lone Ranger" of succession planning. He is only one person playing on an entire team. Granted, he is an important player, but he is not the only player.

---

[51] Russell, pp. 62-63.

Who, then, are the other players? The answer is determined by your congregation's polity (i.e., internal structure). It may be that you are a part of a denomination, and transition planning is not the responsibility of the local church, whatsoever. A regional official of the denomination may make the decision as to when the long tenured pastor leaves and who replaces him. Or it may be that your church functions with a traditional church board, and they serve at the succession planning team; or it may be that your church is led by a team of Elders, who would then comprise the succession planning team. Still, your church leaders may select individuals to serve just in this specific capacity. That being the case, you may wish to name the team so that they have an appropriate identity. Rather than brand them with the word succession, you may want to call them the Leadership Continuity Team (LCT), as they will be devoted to the sole purpose of insuring that a God-honoring transition happens, insuring that continual leadership will be provided for the local church. The LCT could be comprised of a few of the Elders, appropriate staff, lay leaders from the church, and the retiring pastor. Whoever is chosen and appointed to this task must realize that they are a part of a team of people who want to win at the game of succession, realizing that this is not a game. Moreover, these individuals must be willing to work alongside the exiting leader as he leads the process, and he must do so with authentic humility with only the best interest of the church in mind.

Russell contends that the senior minister initiates the process, whereas Bill Hybels is of the opinion that it can be either the exiting leader or the Church Board. In an extensive interview on Willow Creek Association's "Defining Moments,"

Hybels indicated that either party can initiate the process, yet two of the most important issues in jump starting the development of a succession plan are the tenure and age of the pastor. Hybels firmly stated that if the exiting leader has been at the helm for more than twenty years and is the mid-to-late fifties, this conversation must be taking place. If the exiting leader fails to bring it up, he maintains that the Church Board must bring it up. Likewise, if the Church Board does not make mention of a necessary leader><shift, then the exiting pastor must initiate the planning process.

Further, Bill Hybels believes that the planning stage should be as unemotional as possible, making every effort to keep the conversation friendly and as low key as possible. There should be no hidden agendas on anyone's mind, and the only motivation in having these conversations is simply the well-being of the local church or parachurch organization. This initial conversation will not result in a completed succession plan, but will open the door to continuing dialogue. The leadership team that formulates the plan must agree to bring it up in regular conversation, and with increasing frequency with the aging of the exiting leader.[52]

Push pause.
Who will start the succession planning process in your church or ministry—and when? Who will be on your LCT (Leadership Continuity Team), and who will lead your team?

---

[52] Bill Hybels. Defining Moments Interview #1304: "Your Church's Next Leader" Interview. Barrington, IL: Willow Creek Association.

JESUS AND HIS TEAM

While on earth, Jesus enjoyed a relationship rich life. Using the diagram below and starting at the bottom left, notice that Jesus had occasional contact with the most number of people (i.e., the multitudes), such as when He preached the Sermon on the Mount or multiplied the fish and the loaves. As we move up the left side of the triangle, we notice that the numbers of people with whom Jesus did life began to decrease. For example, there was a large group of people who met with Jesus when He appeared to five hundred believers following His resurrection (see 1 Corinthians 15:6). He spent more time training and equipping seventy-two of His followers before sending them out two-by-two (see Luke 10:1, 17). Yet, Jesus spent the majority of His time with the twelve disciples. For a little over three years, Jesus invested His life in developing their lives. He was counting on these men to take His good news to others. Even out of these twelve, Jesus spent unique moments with the inner circle—James, Peter and John—as when He took them to 1) the top of the Mount of Transfiguration, 2) to witness the healing of Jairus' daughter, and 3) to pray with Him in the Garden of Gethsemane the night prior to His death. Jesus was part of a team of twelve men; men that He had coached and mentored to change the world following His death and resurrection—and they did.

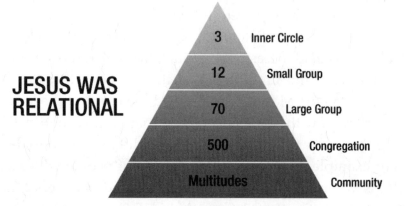

In much the same way, we are to be relational. Beginning at the bottom right corner of the triangle, consider that we have occasional contact with "multitudes" in that we are a part of a larger community in which we live. Then, moving up the right side of the triangle, we notice that the quantity of people with whom we have contact begins to lessen. We spend some amount of our time in worship with people in the congregation we serve. We may be in a part of a large group, such as a men's ministry team in the church that meets periodically. Yet, we may spend the most amount of our time with only a few people, such as those in our small group. This could be an in home Bible study for couples, a men's small group Bible study, etc. These are the individuals with whom we are spending the majority of our time in Christian community. Yet, like Jesus, we must have an inner circle of men with whom to do life, and it is in this inner circle that we experience the deepest of Christian brotherhood and accountability. A great place to find such friends is on the Elder Team, and the Elder Team just might serve as the LCT: Leadership Continuity Team.

TEAM HEALTH

Because effective transitions are of vital importance in any organization, the leadership team responsible for this initiative must be as healthy as possible. In his book *The Advantage: Why Organizational Health Trumps Everything Else in Business*, Patrick Lencioni writes that there are smart organizations in that they have perfected their strategy, marketing, finance and technology areas of business. Yet, Lecioni contends that some organizations have "the advantage" in that not only are they smart, but that they are healthy. Healthy organizations have five traits: 1) minimal politics, 2) minimal confusion, 3) high morale, 4) high productivity, and 5) low turnover.[53] A stronger, healthier succession leadership team will have a greater likelihood of directing an effective transition.

Think 'team' with me. When it comes to a golf team, the players go off and play the game on their own and when finished, their individual scores are added up at the end of the tournament to determine which team won the game. Regretfully, we often act and play like a golf team. We go off and do our own thing in ministry within the local church, and then we occasionally come together to see how we are doing in this thing we call ministry leadership. Yet, we should look and act more like a football or basketball team. On those teams, the athletes play simultaneously together. The players interact with one another; depend on one other during the play, all in hopes of moving the ball down the field for a touchdown or to

---

[53] Patrick Lencioni, *The Advantage: Why Organizational Health Trumps Everything Else in Business* (San Francisco: Jossey-Bass, 2012), pp. 5-6.

the other end of the court for a basket. To be a healthy LCT (Leadership Continuity Team), we have to work together and not apart from one another.

So, how do we become a healthy team? For that matter, what does a healthy team look like? Where do we find such answers? By far, the best resource for our teams that work together in ministry is found in the Word of God. When Jesus Christ was nearing His death, resurrection and ascension (i.e., His transition), He modeled three vital signs of a healthy team for us to emulate with our teams. When we arrive for our appointment at the doctor's, a nurse will check our vital signs: blood pressure, pulse and temperature. As we move through a few passages from the Gospel of Mark, assess the health of your LCT. Determine to what degree your team models these three vital signs of health.

Before identifying these three health components, we must first consider the structure of the Gospel of Mark, where the vital signs are found. This New Testament book is in the shape of a large V. Moving from the top of the V, chapters 1-7 describe the three years of Christ's ministry, which is forty-four percent of the Gospel. Moving downward, chapters 8-10 describe the final six months of Christ's ministry, which is nineteen percent of the Gospel; while as we near the bottom of the V, chapters 11-16 describe the final week in the life of Jesus, comprising thirty-seven percent of the content in Mark.

103

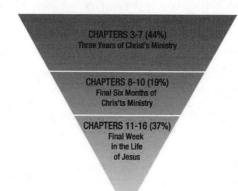

The gospel of Mark grows more intense as we move from beginning to end, and midway through this Gospel—in chapters 7 and 8—we discover four vital signs of team health that Jesus practiced with His disciples as He neared His transition out of leadership and away from this earth.

Mark 8:31-38

He then began to teach them that the Son of Man must suffer many things and be rejected by the Elders, chief priests and teachers of the law, and that he must be killed and after three days rise again. He spoke plainly about this, and Peter took him aside and began to rebuke him. But when Jesus turned and looked at his disciples, he rebuked Peter. "Get behind me, Satan!" he said. "You do not have in mind the things of God, but the things of men." Then he called the crowd to him along with his disciples and said: "If anyone would come after me, he must deny himself and take up his cross and follow me. For whoever wants to save his life will lose it, but whoever loses his life for me and for the gospel will save it. What good is it for a man to gain the whole world, yet forfeit his soul? Or what can a man give in exchange for his soul? If anyone is ashamed of me and my words in this adulterous and sinful generation, the Son of Man will be ashamed of him when he comes in his Father's glory with the holy angels."

The disciples had a limited view of who Jesus was and why He came. They believed that He was the Messiah, but in their minds, the Messiah would lead a military victory over the Roman occupation, restoring Israel as a sovereign nation. The Messiah was a victorious conqueror, but again He told His team that He would be rejected by the Jews and then killed. In their thinking, Messiahs don't die. Peter was so confused over this that he rebuked Jesus for speaking about dying. They failed to see the big picture. Their perspective was limited and poor. Jesus was teaching them an important vital sign of a healthy team: a healthy team knows and pursues the mission.

As discussed in chapter four, Jesus stayed on mission. He had one primary mission, not three or four; but only one, and that was to seek and to save what was lost. He never lost sight of His primary mission. A healthy team knows and pursues that same mission, with everything else being secondary. As the LCT directs the leader><shift of the church, they must stay focused on this one primary mission.

Mark 9:30-32
They left that place and passed through Galilee. Jesus did not want anyone to know where they were, because

he was teaching his disciples. He said to them, "The Son of Man is going to be betrayed into the hands of men. They will kill him, and after three days he will rise." But they did not understand what he meant and were afraid to ask him about it.

Jesus was teaching His team, and the word "teaching" is in a tense of Greek indicating that He kept teaching and teaching and teaching His team. He never did stop training and equipping them. A second vital sign of a healthy team is that it is continually in training. The LCT must have a teachable spirit, wanting to learn from other organizations as to how they directed an effective succession. The team will read available books and articles on succession planning, while attending webinars and seminars on the same subject.

A school system rises to a level of effectiveness equal to that of the faculty and administration leading the school. A business corporation rises to a level of effectiveness equal to that of its board of directors and senior leadership team. A military rises to a level of effectiveness equal to that of its senior officers. A church rises to a level of effectiveness equal to that of her leadership. Likewise, the success of our succession plan is in direct proportion to the level of our leadership skills. If we lack such skills to lead in this specific task, we must be teachable in spirit and willing to continually learn how to make an effective transition. Echoing the sentiment of the late President Harry Truman, "the buck stops here." We, the Leadership Continuity Team, accepts full responsibility to direct a successful succession, and for that to happen, we need to be continually trained for the task.

This vital sign is captured all the more clearly in another moment near the end of Christ's life. After Jesus and His inner circle came down from the top of the Mount of Transfiguration, He noticed a commotion among the people. Asking a few questions, He quickly found out that the other nine guys on His team had failed in ministry. A father had brought his young son to the disciples to be healed of a demonic spirit, and the disciples failed at fulfilling that request. Taking matters into His own hands, Jesus said...

Mark 9:19
"O unbelieving generation," Jesus replied, "how long shall I stay with you? How long shall I put up with you? Bring the boy to me."

This is one of those tough sayings of Jesus. Don't think for a moment that Jesus was meek and mild. Jesus had a strong, even wild side to Him. He was a carpenter who wore jeans and had a lunch pail clutched in His calloused hands. He didn't walk around in a flowing white robe, with perfectly brushed hair in place, while carrying fresh flowers to give away. Jesus had a wild side to Him, and this was one of the moments when we hear just one of the hard sayings of Jesus. This comment had to have ripped right into the heart, mind and souls of His team. Those guys had to have felt both embarrassed and ashamed for their failure. Notice what then happened.

Mark 9:28-29

After Jesus had gone indoors, his disciples asked him privately, "Why couldn't we drive it out?" He replied, "This kind can come out only by prayer."

Once they were behind closed doors, His guys were teachable in spirit. Once they were alone, they had an honest, transparent conversation among themselves. They wanted to know why they failed, and Jesus told them. When He answered their question with, "This kind can come out only by prayer," He inferred that they had failed to pray. We cannot stress sufficiently the need to be teachable in spirit. Our LCT must model a humble, teachable attitude in that directing a transition may be completely new to us. We've never had a leader><shift under our watch, so we need to learn how to maneuver through the uncharted territory of succession. Be teachable.

Mark 9:33-35

They came to Capernaum. When he was in the house, he asked them, "What were you arguing about on the road?" But they kept quiet because on the way they had argued about who was the greatest. Sitting down, Jesus called the Twelve and said, "If anyone wants to be first, he must be the very last, and the servant of all."

Remember the context of this passage. Jesus is getting very close to the time of His death, and He had to have been disappointed in His team, particularly in their attitude. With only weeks remaining until His crucifixion, the disciples of

Jesus were still arguing as to who was the greatest among them. His team struggled with pride and arrogance. The men on His team were full of themselves, and Jesus called them on it. A third and final vital sign of team health is humility. We previously determined that a healthy team is teachable, but the team will never be teachable unless it is first a humble team. Humility is missing from the American culture, and more specifically, it is missing from our lives. When people do not keep a check on pride or arrogance, it diminishes team health.

Did you ever play King of the Hill when you were growing up? Having grown up along the shores of Lake Michigan, we had a lot of snow in which to play. When the plows came through, they pushed the snow into piles that were enormously high. As soon as the snow plows were gone, we climbed to the top of the snow piles and began playing king of the hill. The object of the game was to throw all the other kids off the top of the hill. Do I need to tell you that I loved playing that game? I had to be king of the hill. Regretfully, that same attitude can surface from deep within me today, and perhaps in you. When we have to be number one, first in every category of life, we tend to do whatever it takes to be king of the hill in life. It is time to stop playing games and pursue humility because "God opposes the proud, but gives grace to the humble" (James 4:6).

Why would God oppose pride? Could it be that it was the very first sin ever committed, destroying the purity of His creation? Adam and Eve committed the second sin, second only to the rebellion of Satan when he, and a host of angels, wanted to be like God. Their cardinal sin began the great moral fall of humanity. Pride competes with God for supremacy. Pride lifts us up when God should be the One lifted up. In James 4:6 ("God opposes the proud..."), the word oppose is a present tense, active verb in Greek, meaning that God's opposition to pride is both immediate and continual. We do not want God opposing or working against us. Together, we must ask God to forgive us of our pride, but also for strength to repent of pride. When every individual on our Leadership Continuity Team is authentically humble in spirit, the team will be healthy. Strive to stay on mission, while being both teachable and humble; for in doing so, the team will be healthy and strong, particularly for accomplishing the demanding task given them.

Eleven miles off the east coast of Scotland, out into the frigid waters of the North Sea, stands Bell Rock Lighthouse (http://www.bellrock.org.uk/). It has endured the ferocious onslaught of the North Sea's violent storms since 1811. It rests on less than an acre of solid rock. That small reef is covered by sea water twenty hours a day. Robert Stevenson, the builder of the lighthouse, and his crew of sixty-five men had only four hours a day to work feverously away at the stone, gouging a deep foundation into the rock with their hand tools. As a result of their intentional effort, the one hundred fifteen foot tall lighthouse is still in use today, saving the lives of many people from crashing onto the reef.

Likewise for us, time may be short. The time allotted our Leadership Continuity Team may be passing before our very eyes as the window of opportunity to successfully direct a transition decreases. With every passing day, it is becoming increasingly apparent that a necessary ending must take place sooner than later. Work feverously as a team to get the job done.

Push pause.
Like a nurse taking your vital signs, determine the health of your Leadership Continuity Team (LCT) in three essential areas: 1) do you each know and pursue your one primary mission as a church; 2) are you teachable in spirit; and 3) are you practicing humility?

Part III
The Process

Reality #9:
Think Relay Race

"In the presence of God and of Christ Jesus, who will judge the living and the dead, and in view of His appearing and His kingdom, I give you this charge: Preach the Word..."
2 Timothy 4:1-2

Like many Americans, I enjoy the Olympics. When the summer or winter games are taking place, I will watch hours of the television coverage. Over the years, certain Olympic moments are well remembered, such as what happened at the 2008 summer games in Beijing. Both USA men and women's 4x100 relay teams were serious contenders for medals, but both teams failed to make it past the semi-finals. The improbable happened. Both teams were disqualified when runners dropped the baton while attempting to hand it off to the anchor runners.

A relay race serves as a strong metaphor for succession because we do the improbable, often dropping the baton of leadership when attempting to hand it off to the next generation. Still, there is much more from this race metaphor to grasp. Having run some marathons, I enjoy running and have been coached through the years by some gifted athletes. One coach, in particular, has fielded a number of 4x100 relay teams and offers us many insights when it comes to winning a relay race; and if we look long and hard at the relay metaphor, it speaks volumes into succession planning.

113

UNDERSTANDING A RELAY RACE

In track and field, relay races are exciting events, and for that reason, many track meets save the relay race for the last event of the meet. It is surprising to many people that the fastest team is not always the winning team. Teams that develop a strong race strategy and effectively pass the baton can take home the winner's medal.

First, a winning race strategy involves putting athletes in the best running order. Typically, the second fastest runner leads off in the race, followed by the third fastest runner taking the second leg of the event, who is then followed by the slowest runner in the third leg, while the fastest runner on the team serves as the anchor runner in the fourth and final leg. These four athletes must train for and run the race in a spirit of complete unity, acknowledging that each runner brings unique ability to the event. All four runners work in tandem with one another and not competitively against one another. When one runner finishes his respective leg, he cheers on the athletes running after him. He doesn't berate his teammates; he cheers them on to the finish line. The focus is on winning the race, and not on out-performing your teammates.

A second winning strategy involves the baton exchange. There is much to consider if the team hopes to make the exchange effectively. First, the baton must be handed off in what is called the exchange zone, a twenty meter portion of the running lane. The receiving runner must begin running before receiving the baton. While he can start running outside of the zone, the exchange must happen within the zone. For this to happen, the incoming runner must be running at peak speed. He cannot slow down. The exchange happens most effectively

114

when made midway through the zone. Neither runner is allowed to step outside of the exchange lane. Moreover, the baton cannot be tossed to the next runner, as both runners must have their hands on the baton while making the exchange.

There are two primary methods of exchange: blind and visual exchanges. The blind exchange method requires a great deal of cooperation and practice between the runners because they are making the exchange using voice commands. Without looking back for the approaching runner, the receiving runner begins running and when the incoming runner is ready to hand off the baton, he yells, "Stick!" The voice command prompts the receiving runner to reach back his hand to receive the baton. It is vitally important for the receiving runner to recognize the voice of his teammate. Other runners on other teams are yelling, "Stick!" It is not uncommon for a failed exchange to happen when a runner listens to the wrong voice. This method, when perfected, can win the race for the team. Yet, when a visual exchange method is used the receiving runner looks over his shoulder to see the incoming runner, which can result in a slower starting speed for this leg of the race.

These are but some of the ideas to consider if teams want to win a relay race. Not only must they play by the rules, but they must think and run strategically the moment they take the field. They run to win.

MEANING FROM THE METAPHOR

In Part Two of *Leader><Shift*, we explored issues that cause us to think of the need to develop a written succession plan; and once the written plan is in place, there will come a

day when it must be put into action. On the day we push the plan's proverbial start button, we initiate the succession process. Part Three of *Leader><Shift* introduces a number of process issues that should stir our thinking. This chapter introduces the issues we face in the actual process of making the transition; issues that are conspicuously noticeable in the relay race metaphor. No matter the size of the church or parachurch organization involved in transition, the following process issues must be thoroughly discussed and explored by the succession leadership team.

The Issue of a United Team

Runners on the relay team do not compete against one another, and the same must be true about leaders within the church or ministry organization, whether they are on the paid staff or serve as volunteer. There must be a spiritually and relationally united team involved in the actual succession process. Just as there are four runners on the relay team, consider the four unique 'runners' involved in the transition: the exiting leader, the incoming leader, the staff, and the Elders (i.e., laity leaders in your ministry setting). These four parties must work well together once the process begins. If not, there is little hope that the succession will be successful. The attitude and actions of the exiting leader must be God honoring and humble; while the attitudes and actions of the incoming leader must be the same. Both of these individuals are discussed in greater detail in Part Four. Likewise, the staff of the church or parachurch organization can be unsettled during the transition, particularly given that they may sense little or no job security. The staff plays a vital role in succession, and if they are not relationally healthy with other team members, their attitude and actions can derail this process. Finally, the Elders fulfill an essential role in succession. If they micro-manage this process and do not allow the exiting pastor to be highly involved, there is little chance for an effective transition. If Elders superimpose their authority over staff who are trying to lead the church through this challenging time, tension will result and a baton of leadership may be dropped. Each of the four parties must sincerely want what is best for one another, the local church, and for the kingdom of God. Like runners on the track, they must cheer one another on to victory, affirming that this process is not about any individual or groups of people, but about bringing honor to God.

The Issue of Timing

The transfer of a relay baton must happen in a twenty meter exchange zone. In much the same way, there must be a stated period of time when the actual leadership exchange will take place. If the 'exchange zone' is too long, the congregation or organization will experience what can be called exhaustive anticipation: the perpetual waiting for the exiting leader to exit. If the exchange zone is too brief, the congregation or organization can experience what is called leadership whiplash: the abrupt and painful change of ministry direction.

For some churches and organizations, the incoming leader may already be on staff, which will shorten the time needed to make the transition, but do not think or act with haste. Though the incoming leader has been found internally, an effective leader><shift with an internal candidate must involve mentoring by the exiting leader, gradual assumption of

117

leadership responsibility among the staff, and more. When the incoming leader is found through external means, the length of time for the transition is longer. At The Creek, we work extensively with three year strategic plans and one possible scenario for the timing of our succession is for the process to start at the beginning of a three year cycle and I will exit before the end of that three year strategic plan.

Another issue that affects the timing issue is the size of the church or parachurch organization. The larger the ministry, the longer it will take to complete a succession process. Accomplished pilots will land a Cessna 172 in a grassy landing strip only fifteen hundred feet long, whereas pilots of a fully loaded 747 jumbo jet need between nine thousand and twelve thousand feet of runway. The larger the plane, the longer the runway that is needed for a safe take-off or landing. The larger the church or ministry organization, the longer the period of time needed for an effective transition. It is reasonable to assume that larger churches have more complex issues, which require the incoming pastor to be a high capacity leader. These organizations of scale have unique leadership demands and finding a capable leader will require more time.

The Issue of Pace

Just as the incoming runner must increase his speed as he approaches the exchange zone, the exiting pastor must do the same. All too often, ministers approaching retirement begin to slow down and coast to the finish. They have diminishing energy and creative ability. Slowing down is not a part of a healthy and successful transition. The exiting leader cannot mentally check out or become a lame duck. He must continue to intentionally lead, particularly by example. He must lead the congregation by humbly affirming his successor in sincere and practical ways. Until his final day, he must lead by having conversations with staff, expressing his appreciation for their past support and involvement in ministry, while thanking them for their future support and service alongside their new leader. These same conversations can—and must—happen with groups of people, teams of people and individuals throughout the church. Moreover, the exiting leader must have conversations with individuals and organizations that are in partnership with the church externally for the purpose of introducing and affirming his successor in the expanded sphere of influence of the church. All of these necessary conversations take time, and demand that the exiting leader keep pace. This is no time to slow down and check out.

The Issue of Listening to Wrong Voices

Runners train themselves to distinguish the voices of their teammates. We must do the same. When the succession process begins and it becomes all the more apparent to people that the long tenured pastor is leaving, a crescendo of comments will be heard from people. Some individuals will contact their beloved pastor and plead with him to stay, even though he knows it is time to go. These voices are appreciated, but they are wrong all the same. Other voices will be heard as to who on the staff team needs to become the successor. Some of those voices will speak out of appreciation for an individual, but not in respect to the individual's capacity to lead or calling. These voices are often wrong. Some voices will be heard

119

saying that they do not like the new succession plan that has been initiated by the leadership, and that they want to return to the old way of finding a pastor. In those instances, the church must move forward with a new plan for a new day (Chapter 6), even to the dislike of some individuals. If we listen to voices of dissent, we will find ourselves listening to the wrong voices. In 1 Kings 12:1-24, a leader><shift took place between King Solomon and his son, Rehoboam. In the midst of the transition, the new king asked advice of both Israel's Elders and of his young peers. Rehoboam listened to the wrong voices, and as a result, Israel was divided by a civil war that raged on for decades until both the northern and southern kingdoms were defeated by invading armies and carried off into exile. Listening to the wrong voices in times of transition can cause indescribable loss for years to come.

The Issue of the Lane

When runners are exchanging the baton, they cannot step out of their respective lanes. Teammates must both be in the same lane throughout the exchange. In much the same manner, the successor must move the church or organization forward in the same direction his predecessor was leading. For the succession process to be effective, leaders must have clearly stated the vision, mission and core values for the church or organization. The vision is the dream we want the come true; the mission is how we hope to make the dream come true; while the core values are the operating system of the church or organization. Once these foundational issues are in place, the church can begin developing and using three year strategic planning, and such a plan should be in place when the incoming leader arrives on the scene. As stated in Chapter 4 Stay on Mission, the incoming leader must embrace the stated vision and direction of the church, as established by the leadership. Though he is now driving the proverbial bus, the successor must drive according to the GPS established prior to his arrival. In *Start With Why*, author Simon Sinek provides specific examples of incoming CEOs who embraced a different vision for their organizations than what their successful predecessors pursued. The organizations they were called to lead began to suffer because the successor did not lead the organization in the same direction. Momentum slowed. Tensions flared. Profits declined. An incoming leader who changes the direction of the church while in the midst of the succession process is asking for trouble. During the exchange, stay in the same lane and humbly head in the same direction.

The Issue of Not Tossing the Baton

Finally, runners must hand the baton to one another, they cannot throw or toss it. With care and precision, they must exchange the baton hand-to-hand. Likewise, with care and precision, we must pass the baton of leadership to the next generation. The succession process cannot be pursued carelessly, as in tossing or throwing a relay baton. This process is of critical importance to those involved, including the congregation or constituents of the parachurch organization. As stated in Chapter 3, God has given us a trust and we must prove faithful. Expedite the succession with serious intent. The church or ministry we lead is not ours, but God's.

At the beginning of this chapter, words appear from the end of the Apostle Paul's life. While sitting on death row in a

121

Roman prison awaiting his execution, Paul handed the baton of pastoral leadership to Timothy, his adopted son in the faith. Their exchange zone was packed with painful emotion as it involved saying good-bye to one another from a distance. We do not know if Timothy and Paul ever saw one another again prior to the execution, though Paul pleaded with Timothy in his letter to come quickly to him. Moreover, a conspicuous solemnity and seriousness marked their exchange zone: "In the presence of God and of Christ Jesus...I give you this charge..." When in the exchange zone, while handing over the baton of leadership to the next generation, recognize and appreciate the emotional and spiritual depth of the process. While the exchange must be honoring to God, it can and should be life changing for us.

Push pause.
While in your final season of ministry (i.e., running your lap in the relay), rank order—from most to least important—the relay race metaphors as they relate to your ministry setting:

- o Having a united team
- o Making the exchange at the right time
- o Keeping and increasing leadership pace
- o Not listening to the wrong voice
- o The successor embracing the same vision, mission and values
- o Carefully handing leadership to the next generation

Reality #10:
Attitude and Appreciation are
Needed

"Don't let anyone look down on you because you are young,
but set an example for the believers in speech, in life, in love,
in faith and in purity."
1 Timothy 4:12

When we first drove up to take a look the massive pipe, we were stunned. Our family vacation that summer took us into the interior of Alaska, and we were awestruck at the enormity of the Trans-Alaska Pipeline. Measuring four feet in diameter, the pipeline extends eight hundred miles from Prudhoe Bay in the north, all the way south to the oil terminal on Prince William Sound in the city of Valdez. Built above the ground due to the dangers of permafrost, our family was able to follow the pipeline well into the Arctic Circle, across hundreds of miles of tundra. Yet, when we toured the oil storage and shipping complex at Valdez, we learned a startling fact: the pipeline is running far from capacity.

When it opened in 1977, the Trans-Alaska Pipeline was an engineering marvel of the twentieth century. More than seventy-thousand people worked on the line, completing it in three years as a solution to the oil crisis of 1973. Once open, it took only months for the oil to begin flowing freely from frozen Artic in the north into the cavernous oil tankers waiting at their berths in the south. Today, engineers believe that the pipeline is at risk; not from sabotage or permafrost, but from dwindling

123

amounts of oil being transported through the pipe. A minimum capacity of oil is needed to maintain a certain oil temperature, and if the temperature falls too low, the danger of ice and wax accumulation can cause serious damage to the pipeline. Oil production peaked in 1988 when the pipeline transported 2.1 million barrels of oil per day, yet it has been declining every year since. Now, there are some days when barely half a million barrels of crude flow south to the oil terminal at Valdez. The Trans-Alaska Pipeline operates at one-third of its capacity, and if it continues to decrease, it can become both uneconomical and unsafe to operate. From this vacationer's perspective, it looks like the pipeline is running dry.[54]

THE LEADERSHIP PIPELINE

There is another pipeline failing to run at capacity, and in some places, the pipeline is bone dry. It is the leadership pipeline. When we consider the many churches and parachurch organizations needing leaders, one would conclude that the leadership pipeline is running dry. Congregations find it increasingly difficult to fill volunteer leadership positions in the local church. Moreover, churches discover that it is equally a challenge to find leaders for paid ministry staff positions. Gone are the days when the posting of a ministry opening would be answered by dozens, if not hundreds, of resumes. Why is that? Could it be that the leadership pipeline is not running at capacity? Where are the next generation leaders? Who will serve the ever increasing vacancies created by aging

---

[54] http://www.popularmechanics.com/science/energy/coal-oil-gas/how-much-life-is-left-in-the-trans-alaska-pipeline

and retiring leaders, serving both on staff and as volunteers? Could it be that next generation leaders have little or no interest to serve in a church or ministry organization?

The books *Unchristian* (2007) and *You Lost Me* (2011), authored by David Kinnaman, explore the attitudes of sixteen to twenty-nine year-olds in relation to the Christian faith. Kinnaman's research findings were nothing less than eye opening. Due to a variety of well-documented reasons, increasing numbers of individuals from the next generation want little or nothing to do with Christianity. Fewer young people are converting to Christianity, and this makes for a shrinking pool of young prospective students to attend Christian universities and seminaries to prepare for vocational ministry. That being the case, it stands to reason that the leadership pipeline is running at a significantly reduced capacity, which makes it difficult to fill paid and volunteer leadership vacancies.

The fact that there are fewer people in the leadership pipeline is further aggravated by the low retention rate among those who are currently serving in ministry. When I was completing my doctoral degree, I was privileged to have Dr. H.B. London, of Focus on the Family, as a professor. Dr. London shared results from research conducted by Focus that indicated as many as one of every two ordained ministers was leaving the ministry by their tenth anniversary of ordination. Again, for a variety of reasons, ministers were then—and still are—abandoning their call to the pastorate in record numbers, which creates even more vacancies to fill. Something must be done to address this crisis.

The Trans-Alaska Pipeline was not the only engineering marvel of the twentieth century. That century was ushered in by what the American Society of Civil Engineers has called one of the engineering projects of the millennium. In the late 1800s, the Chicago River was a shallow, slow moving sewer for the struggling metropolis of Chicago. Animal waste from the Union Stock Yards flowed into the river, along with factory and human waste. The river was actually combustible and contributed to the horrific loss attributed to the Great Chicago Fire of 1871. This never-ending flow of waste dumped directly into Lake Michigan, which was Chicago's source of drinking water. As a result, disease was rampant throughout the city, causing the deaths of over ten thousand people annually from typhoid fever and cholera through the 1880s and 1890s. In 1885 alone, just shy of one hundred thousand people died of water borne illnesses.

City engineers did what seemed impossible. Digging more than twenty-eight miles of canal and moving more earth and rock than originally moved in building the Panama Canal, a system of locks and gates were built; and on January 2, 1900, a worker opened a gate that flooded the canal system with water pouring in from Lake Michigan. At once, the water of the Chicago River was struck head on by the torrential water of the Great Lake, reversing the actual flow of the river! Now flowing in an opposite direction, the Chicago River emptied into the Mississippi River basin and out into the Gulf of Mexico. Fresh water brought new and abundant life to what could have been a dying city on the American landscape, but a decision to intentionally reverse the direction of the river brought an end to a threatening crisis.[55] In much the same manner, an intentional change of direction needs to take place in our attitude and thinking if the process of succession is to be effective.

> *Push pause.*
> Describe the leadership pipeline at your church or in your ministry. How would you rate the current capacity—full and overflowing with new and upcoming leaders, or bone dry without any potential leaders being prepared? What contributes to or detracts from the flow of your leadership pipeline?

A NEW APPRECIATION

The New Testament paints a vivid picture of the power of the attitudes of people towards others. In Acts 16:1-2, the Apostle Paul met—for the first time—a young man by the name of Timothy. This is the Timothy who became Paul's "adopted son in the faith." It is not surprising that Paul seriously considered taking Timothy as a ministry protégé when we consider the details of verse 2, where ten simple words state: "The believers at Lystra and Iconium spoke well of him." A plurality of people (i.e., "brothers") in a plurality of places (i.e., "Lystra and Iconium") spoke well of Timothy. Multiple believers in multiple places did not speak derisively of young Timothy. To the contrary, they spoke well of him. They appreciated the young man. Not only did they have a right and good attitude towards him, but they highly recommended

---

[55] http://www.greatlakeswaterwars.com/chapter5.htm

him to Paul, who took him under wing and mentored him as a spiritual father.

Yet, having people speak highly of him was not always what Timothy experienced. Some years later, Timothy experienced quite the opposite. There were a number of believers who did not appreciate Timothy, nor did they have a right attitude towards him. Who were they? These were troubled church members in "First Christian Church" of Ephesus. The Apostle Paul had served as the pastor in Ephesus for three years (Acts 20:31), and then tendered his resignation to the Elders of the church (Acts 20:17-38). While speaking to the Elders, Paul prophesied that some from their very own number would become false teachers in order to "draw people after them" (Acts 20:30). When Paul left Ephesus, he was replaced by Timothy. His son in the faith became the pastor of the troubled church. It should not surprise us that Ephesus was spiritually struggling because Paul's prophesy came to be true. In 1 Timothy 1:3, Paul urged Timothy to "stay there in Ephesus and command certain men not to teach false doctrines any longer." Who were the men teaching false doctrine? They were the Elders at Ephesus.

Now imagine this picture. Young Timothy is the pastor of what was considered one of the largest congregations numbered among the first century churches, yet it was a highly dysfunctional church because the Elders were teaching twisted doctrine. No wonder Timothy wanted to leave, and we know he did because Paul urged him to stay put. Though Timothy was ready to update his resume, Paul urged him to stay and lead the difficult people. It is of no surprise to us that Paul also urged Timothy to "use a little wine because of your stomach and frequent illnesses" (1 Timothy 5:23). Having to correct the Elders of the church was making Timothy sick to his stomach. Perhaps he had ulcers from the stress of the situation. Moreover, the Apostle Paul wrote: "Don't let anyone look down on you because you are young, but set an example for the believers in speech, in conduct, in love, in faith and in purity" (1 Timothy 4:12). Why would Paul write such a thing? There were Christians in the church at Ephesus who had a judgmental attitude towards Timothy and they "looked down on him" in a derisive manner. That is not surprising being that a young pastor had to correct and reprimand the spiritual behavior of the Elders of the church. Imagine the gossip that would have ensued and the backstabbing of a young man simply attempting to lead the church in a way that would honor God. The Ephesus church was in the midst of a succession process, and it was not going well because of the poor attitude of those who were older towards their new pastor, who happened to be younger.

Sound familiar? How many stories can we tell of congregations where the young, new pastor was not appreciated by those who were older? All too often, the attitude towards next generation leaders is not one of appreciation and affirmation. This is not only true in the American Church culture, but poor attitudes towards younger leaders is common in church cultures around the world. Teaching as an adjunct for Christian seminaries, I have personally met young ministers in many different nations who have been treated disrespectfully by the older generation. Many of these young men have left the ministry and have transitioned into secular career paths, wanting nothing more to do with being a pastor. As noted earlier in this chapter, roughly half of the pastors in America are leaving the ministry by the tenth anniversary of their ordination, many of whom are young—and we wonder why the leadership pipeline is running dry.

If the direction of the Chicago River can be changed, we can certainly change the direction of our attitudes towards next generation leaders. Rather than resent them, we can respect them and deliberately turn to them in consideration of leading in our place. It is time to stop judging the next generation and finding fault with them. Rather, we need to turn to them in hopes that they will actually do more to advance the kingdom of God than we only dreamed of doing. That sentiment is taught in the Old Testament.

In the Psalms, a familiar passage is often misinterpreted because people fail to grasp the context of the passage before making comment on its content.

Psalm 127:3-5
Sons are a heritage from the LORD, children a reward from him. Like arrows in the hands of a warrior are sons born in one's youth. Blessed is the man whose quiver is full of them. They will not be put to shame when they contend with their enemies in the gate.

People mistake this passage to say that we are all to have a "quiver full" of children—whatever that implies. These verses have nothing to do with the number of children we raise. The context of this passage is about war. There is a warrior with weapons in this passage, and his children are like those weapons in that they will do battle with the enemy at the gate. Remember, cities were attacked at their gates. If gates were broken through, the city and all of its inhabitants could be pillaged. Therefore, the gates were to be protected at all costs. Warriors were stationed above the gates with bows and arrows in hands to send the arrows where the warrior could not go. The warrior did not keep his arrows in his quiver only to admire them. To the contrary, he shot his arrows where he, the warrior, could not go. Our children—those of the next generation—are the arrows. We need next generation leaders to go where we cannot. We must equip, empower and release them to actually advance the kingdom of God in ways we have only hoped of doing, contending with our Enemy at the entry point of our lives. As for myself, I long for the next generation to rise up and be a formidable threat to the kingdom of darkness by leading the Church in bold and decisive ways. They can—and must—do more for the glory of God in making Jesus the Famous One than we ever dreamed possible. This is my heartfelt attitude towards younger leaders in the faith.

Reason with me, Moses wanted to lead the people in the Promised Land and I would venture to think that he had dared to dream of that moment from time to time while walking mile after mile out of Egypt. Yet, that dream would not come true in his life. Joshua, his young successor, actually led the people across the Jordan and into the Promised Land, going where Moses was not meant to go.

The same happened with King David. How he longed to build a temple for God! He had the blueprints drawn up, amassed the building supplies, and was prepared to pay cash for the construction. But, it was not meant for David to do so and his young son and successor Solomon actually accomplished the feat. Even the great prophet Elijah was eclipsed by his young protégé and successor Elisha in that more miracles are recorded and credited to the younger prophet than to his mentor. The night before His death, Jesus said to His disciples: "I tell you the truth, anyone who has faith in Me will do what I have been doing. He will do even greater things than these, because I am going to the Father" (John 14:12). Did Jesus say that His followers then and now would do greater miracles than Him? No. He was referring to the fact that His young followers would have far more time on this earth to do the works that He had been doing, works that would advance the kingdom of God around the world. It would appear that the teaching of Psalm 127:3-5 is seen in one example after another within the Scriptures.

Geoffrey Canada, president and CEO of the Harlem Children's Zone (Harlem, New York), was interviewed by the Willow Creek Association and he made a powerful statement about succession. He challenged his listeners by reminding them that if we attract young, gifted people to replace us, we have to leave or the talented, young leader will leave. He went on to say that if we love the organization we lead, we will leave prior to the moment we burn-out from exhaustion. After all, the organization we lead doesn't belong to us.[56] We will only act on Canada's advice if we have a change of attitude towards those coming behind us.

---

[56] Bill Hybels. Defining Moments Interview #1304: "Your Church's Next Leader" Interview. Barrington, IL: Willow Creek Association.

132

Push pause.

Will we intentionally change our attitudes towards next generation? Will there come a day when we sincerely appreciate them and welcome them into the process of succession, knowing that they will have the opportunity and the capacity to do far more to advance the kingdom of God than we did? To what degree is your church or ministry equipping, empowering and releasing the next generation to lead?

Reality #11:
Change is Inevitable

"Brothers and sisters, choose seven men from among you who are known to be full of the Spirit and wisdom. We will turn this responsibility over to them and will give our attention to prayer and the ministry of the word."
Acts 6:3-4

Thom Rainer and Eric Geiger, in their book *Simple Church*, tell of a medical study that revealed how difficult it is for people to change. An estimated six hundred thousand people undergo heart bypass surgery annually in America. After having lifesaving surgery, these patients understand that they must change the way they live if they hope to continue living because the bypass surgery is only a temporary fix. The recovering patients must change the way they eat, quit smoking and drinking, and add exercise to their daily routines. Their surgeons tell them they need to change the way they live or they will die. Surgery alone cannot save them. The study revealed that two years after having the life-saving surgery, nine out of ten patients had not changed the way they lived. Instead of changing the way they lived, they chose to die.[57]

In much the same way, many leaders in the church and parachurch organizations refuse to change ministry methods, even with regard to leadership transitions. When we refuse to

---

[57] Thom Rainer and Eric Geiger. *Simple Church* (Nashville: Broadman & Holman Publishing Group, 2006), p. 229.

enact appropriate and necessary change, the organization suffers. To be successful with succession, changes will have to be made. For example, after a review of your organization's by-laws, changes may have to be made that will accommodate your new approach to succession planning. Perhaps changes will have to be made to your governance model in order to accomplish the succession plan you designed. If you have decided on a new plan for a new day, changes will have to be made to your old search processes. As you anticipate your long tenured pastor's retirement, changes may have to be made to his financial package, enabling him to retire. Again, your governance documents may need to be changed to allow the new leader to be appointed senior pastor before the current pastor retires. There are a host of questions and situations that prompt possible changes caused by a leader><shift. To prepare for such moments, we need to examine how to make change effectively—something that is modeled for us by the early church.

THE CONTEXT
A Church in Need of Change

In Acts 6:1-7, we read of the church in Jerusalem growing exponentially, and that growth caused significant growing pains.

Verse 1

In those days when the number of disciples was increasing, the Grecian Jews among them complained against the Hebraic Jews because their widows were being overlooked in the daily distribution of food.

"In those days" refers to the early church in her earliest beginnings, a time when the church experienced an increasing number of converts to the faith as the word "increasing" appears in the present tense of Greek, indicating that the action was continuous, never ending. The growing numbers of people in the church caused some significant challenges: Greek speaking widows were being neglected when food was distributed to those in need. The Hebrew speaking widows were getting food, but not Greek speaking widows, and this did not happen only once or twice, but repeatedly (imperfect tense for "overlook"). Some of the widows were well fed, while others were going to bed hungry night after night. This problem was not a one-time occurrence.

This begs us to ask the question why there were so many Greek-speaking widows in Jerusalem in the first place. After all, Jerusalem was the capital city of the Jewish people. Simply put, they wanted to be there. On the Day of Pentecost, tens of thousands of Jewish people were in Jerusalem for the Feast of Pentecost. Acts 2 indicates that when the Holy Spirit was given and the Church was created, three thousand Jewish people came to believe that Jesus was the Messiah. Many of those Jews came from countries in which Greek was spoken as the primary language. Some of those people remained in Jerusalem after Pentecost, enjoying the sense of community described in Acts 2:42-47. Life was exciting because the Church was a dynamic group of people doing life at deep levels of satisfaction, and Greek-speaking widows would have been within that group. Moreover, Hellenistic Jews returned to Jerusalem in their old age, wanting to live out their final days in the Holy City. It appears that there came to be an abundance of Greek-speaking widows in Jerusalem who out lived their husbands.

> Verses 2-4
> So the Twelve gathered all the disciples together and said, "It would not be right for us to neglect the ministry of the word of God in order to wait on tables. Brothers, choose seven men from among you who are known to be full of the Spirit and wisdom. We will turn this responsibility over to them and will give our attention to prayer and the ministry of the word."

The apostles proposed a significant change. They knew they had to do something because the complaining was just a symptom of a far greater problem, that of prejudice. Two ethnic groups were clashing and if ignored, the church could suffer great harm. The leaders did not point a finger of blame at anyone except themselves. They knew they were being stretched too thin, and they were unable to be faithful to their primary calling of prayer and the ministry of the Word (i.e., "ministry" is *diakonia* meaning "to labor"). They wanted to focus their efforts on prayer and making known the Word of God. So, a change had to take place both quickly and effectively as there were hungry widows in their community, who were going to bed hungry night after night.

The first century church was very Jewish in their practices, as seen in this matter. This distribution of food was called the custom of the *kuppah*, a word meaning basket. The apostles had been collecting food and money from people—

going house-to-house—and then giving it to the widows in need. If this benevolent act of kindness were to continue in this rapidly growing church, it required that a change take place. The apostles asked the people to select men known to be full of the Holy Spirit and wisdom, and they would delegate this responsibility to them.

> Verses 5-6
>
> This proposal pleased the whole group. They chose Stephen, a man full of faith and of the Holy Spirit; also Philip, Procorus, Nicanor, Timon, Parmenas, and Nicolas from Antioch, a convert to Judaism. They presented these men to the apostles, who prayed and laid their hands on them.

The people welcomed this change. The men selected to make certain that the Greek speaking widows were fed were Greek men, as they had Greek names. Those men would have been able to speak the language of their widows, but they would also have had a heart of concern for them. The seven men were presented to the apostles, who then prayed over them by laying hands on them. This prayer was one of both blessing and declaration, for in the laying on of hands the apostles gave the team of seven men not on the responsibility, but also the authority to lead in this new compassion based ministry.

Verse 7

So the word of God spread. The number of disciples in Jerusalem increased rapidly, and a large number of priests became obedient to the faith.

There is a particular Greek tense indicating that the Word of God kept spreading; and the number of disciples (i.e., new Christ-followers) kept increasing, even from among the Jewish priests. First century Jewish historian Josephus wrote that there were four tribes of priests; each with an estimated five thousand priests, making for a total of twenty-thousand Jewish priests serving in Jerusalem—and a large number of them became obedient to the Christian faith. Imagine the city-wide impact made when thousands of Jewish priests believed that Jesus was the Messiah. The Word of God continued to spread and the church continued to grow exponentially, due much in part to necessary changes that were made effectively.

THE CONTENT
Making Changes in Today's Church

In light of that text, how do we make change effectively? As we consider this example from the early church, there are insights to follow if we hope to work through necessary changes involved with succession planning. For example, communication was a vital part of the process of resolving the conflict caused by Greek speaking widows not receiving benevolent help. Thorough and clear communication took place between the parties involved. The apostles deliberately engaged the concerned parties impacted by this oversight and they continued their conversation until a resolution was reached. Deeper, more candid conversation helps bring about effective change.

There are five basic levels of communication in our culture: 1) cliché, 2) reporting facts, 3) sharing opinions, 4) sharing feelings, and 5) complete honesty. Levels 1 and 2 are shallow and insignificant. Whereas, real communication begins at level 3 because only then do we risk being rejected by those with whom we are communicating. We must go to greater depths of communicating when attempting significant change. The apostles rightly admitted that they could no longer meet the increasing needs of people, while trying to teach the Word. They were being painfully honest with their admission and sought a much-needed solution, speaking at the deeper levels of conversation.

Consider also that making change effectively requires an open mind. It has been said that one of the hardest things to open is a closed mind. The apostles could have been rigid in their thinking and refused to change their benevolence methods, but if they had, the Greek speaking widows would continue to go hungry and prejudicial tensions would have increased when there should be unity in the church. But, these men were obviously open minded as they quickly invited people to be a part of the solution, which reflects their humility—a virtue worth pursuing.

A non-conventional daredevil has captured the attention of the world. Nik Wallenda, a devout follower of Christ, has become known the world over as a high-wire aerialist. Two recent accomplishments were viewed by over one billion people watching from around the world: walking a tightrope

140

across Niagara Falls in 2012 and becoming the first person to walk a high wire across the Grand Canyon in 2013. These feats are nothing short of spectacular, and Wallenda is aware of his risk at falling from not only a high wire, but as a result of pride. After accomplishing a remarkable feat, Wallenda does something to deliberately humble himself—he picks up trash where the crowds had gathered to watch him.

> "My purpose is simply to help clean up after myself. The huge crowd left a great deal of trash behind, and I feel compelled to pitch in. Besides, after the inordinate amount of attention I sought and received, I need to keep myself grounded. Three hours of cleaning up debris is good for my soul. Humility does not come naturally to me. So if I have to force myself into situations that are humbling, so be it .... I know that I need to get down on my hands and knees like everyone else. I do it because it's a way to keep from tripping. As a follower of Jesus, I see him washing the feet of others. I do it because if I don't serve others I'll be serving nothing but my ego."[58]

If we are to make effective change, it will require open minds. Open minds are the product of humility for only then we will be teachable in spirit. If it is not picking up trash where adoring crowds once stood, what will we intentionally do to pursue humility?

---

[58] Nik Wallenda with David Ritz. *Balance* (New York: Faith Words, 2013), p. 207.

Finally, the apostles made this change in order to remain committed to the purpose of the Church—declaring the Word to reach people for Christ and to teach those in Christ. They were acting on the Great Commission of Jesus Christ to "go and make disciples of all nations," reaching and teaching as they went. They could not do so if they continued to distribute food in the benevolence program. Effective change happens when it is in keeping with the purpose of the Church. Can we say the same? Do we make changes in response to pursuing the primary mission of the Church?

In Luke 9:51, Jesus "resolutely set out for Jerusalem," and began what is known to be His final journey to Jerusalem. He was facing death on a cross, and He let nothing get in His way. In Acts 6, His disciples behaved in much the same manner. They knew their purpose and that was to advance the kingdom of God by making known the Word of God—and they let nothing hinder them in pursuing this grand purpose. When we behave and lead in the same manner, we will make changes that enable us to pursue our mission—and such changes can be made effectively. Communicate. Have open minds. Remain committed to our primary purpose. Then make the change.

Push pause.
With a transition becoming more of a reality, what changes will have to take place in your ministry context? In light of those changes, which of the three elements for making effective change is your weakest: communication, having

an open mind, or remaining committed to the primary purpose of the Church?

RESISTANCE TO CHANGE

Even though we attempt to implement change effectively, there are many people who resist change. In spite of how carefully we proceed with change, there will be those who oppose change. The reasons for resisting change are quite common:

→ The change was not self-initiated.
→ People feel manipulated and lack ownership in the change being made.
→ Their routine is disrupted and people like routines.
→ Change creates fear of the unknown and people do not like insecurity.
→ Change creates fear of failure and people like success more than failure.
→ The purpose of the change is unclear because of poor communication.
→ People like status quo and traditions.
→ Negative thinking prevails; the "can't, won't and don't" mentality reigns.
→ There is a lack of respect and trust in leadership.
→ Change requires additional commitment.

To counter resistance to change, it is essential to create an environment in which change is welcomed and embraced. People do not resist change so much as they resist being changed. In order for changes to occur effectively, a healthy

143

climate or environment must be created within the church or organization among the people. Leaders can create such an environment by pursuing these four initiatives.

First, develop a trust with the people. Building trust requires time. The longer you serve with consistent effectiveness, greater trust is built with people. Trust in leadership creates a climate in which change can be made. Second, leaders must set the example. People need to see the Elders making personal effort in executing change, no matter the cost. We lead by example. The Apostle Paul said to follow his example as he followed the example of Christ (1 Corinthians 11:1). Third, leaders must understand the history of the local church or organization. Change for the future can be made only when we have an appreciation for what happened in the past. Acknowledging and respecting the efforts of people in previous seasons of ministry helps to create a climate for change. Finally, leaders must be able to influence others in a positive way. When inviting others along to "take the hill together", a climate is created that embraces change.

When making decisions that introduce change in the local church, proper timing for implementing the change becomes an issue. There are right and wrong times for implementing change. Here is a check list for making change. These questions can be asked of leadership prior to making a proposed change. By doing so, leaders can determine if now is the right time for the change—or not. When the questions are answered with "yes," the change tends to be easier. Questions answered with "no" usually indicate that the change will be difficult, and perhaps, a bit premature.

144

YES NO

☐ ☐ Will this change benefit the local church or organization?

☐ ☐ Is this change compatible with the purpose of the church?

☐ ☐ Is this change specific and clear?

☐ ☐ Are influential people in favor of the change?

☐ ☐ Is it possible to test this change before making it permanent?

☐ ☐ Is this change reversible?

☐ ☐ Are all the resources available to make this change?

☐ ☐ Is this change the next obvious step?

☐ ☐ Does this change have both short and long range benefit?

☐ ☐ Is the leadership capable of bringing about this change?

☐ ☐ Is the timing right for implementing this change?

Acclaimed authors Dan and Chip Heath, the team of brothers who wrote the best-selling book *Made to Stick: Why Some Ideas Survive and Others Die* (New York: Random House, 2007), told a story about a doctor who urged his colleagues to practice proper hand-washing protocol:

> "[Dr.] Leon Bender became frustrated when he took a South Seas cruise and observed that the crew was more diligent about hand-washing than the staff at his own hospital. Frequent hand-washing by doctors and nurses is one of the best ways to prevent patient infections, and studies estimate that thousands of patients die every

145

year from preventable bacterial infections. Bender and his colleagues tried a variety of techniques to encourage hand-washing, but the staff's compliance with regulations was stuck around 80 percent. Medical standards required a minimum of 90 percent and [his hospital] was due for an inspection from the accrediting board. They had to do better. One day, a committee of 20 doctors and administrators were taken by surprise when, after lunch, the hospital's epidemiologist asked them to press their hands into an agar plate, a sterile Petri dish containing a growth medium. The agar plates were sent to the lab to be cultured and photographed. The photos revealed what wasn't visible to the naked eye: The doctor's hands were covered with gobs of bacteria. Imagine being one of those doctors and realizing that your own hands—the same hands that would examine a patient later in the day, not to mention the same hands that you just used to eat a turkey wrap— were harboring an army of microorganisms. It was revolting. One of the filthiest images in the portfolio was made into a screensaver for the hospital's network of computers ensuring that everyone on staff could share in the horror. Suddenly, hand-hygiene compliance rose to nearly 100 percent and stayed there."[59]

The Heath brothers reached a conclusion that speaks directly into our lives; and that being this: we typically will not change our behavior until we are painfully aware of how we

---

[59] http://www.fastcompany.com/1715064/why-emotion-not-knowledge-catalyst-change

contribute to the problems around us, both in our circumstances and in our relationships. When the succession process begins, necessary changes are inevitable.

Push pause.
Will someone have to confront us with painful truth that we are hurting the process more than helping the process? How do we contribute to the problems associated with a leader><shift, or do we help effect healthy and appropriate change at a defining moment for the ministry we lead?

Part IV

The People

Reality #12:
The Exiting Leader Exits

*"For I am already being poured out like a drink offering
and the time has come for my departure."*
2 Timothy 4:6

While walking through a cemetery and reading gravestones, we are brought to the reality that we enter and exit life. Throughout all of life, we find ourselves making an entrance and an exit. We enter and exit buildings. We do the same for meetings. We enter and exit relationships, while doing the same with different jobs. Life is a series of entering and exiting, so it should not surprise us that there will come a time when we must exit our role as the senior leader.

The Apostle Paul knew that his days were numbered. The fact that the "time had come for (his) departure" did not infer his release from prison on parole. To the contrary, Paul was sitting on death row. He was awaiting his execution. The exemplary leader was about to make his final exit in life and the post-apostolic era of the early church was soon to begin. Younger men would be given the mantle of leadership—men who had not personally met Jesus Christ as had the apostles.

For each of us, there will come a day when we will make our exit. No longer will we serve as the senior leader of the local church or parachurch ministry. We will pack up our books, clean out our desks, and vacate our offices. As we turn in our keys and turn out the lights one last time, our e-mail addresses will be cancelled and the name on our office mail box will be changed. Like it or not, the time will come for our departure. We must make an exit.

Pope Emeritus Benedict XVI vacated his Vatican apartment when he came to the realization that he had to leave the papacy in the hands of a leader, who would be younger and more physically capable than himself. In his letter of resignation to the College of Cardinals, the former pope admitted that it was time to make his exit.

> Dear Brothers,
>
> I have convoked you to this Consistory, not only for the three canonizations, but also to communicate to you a decision of great importance for the life of the Church. After having repeatedly examined my conscience before God, I have come to the certainty that my strengths, due to an advanced age, are no longer suited to an adequate exercise of the Petrine ministry. I am well aware that this ministry, due to its essential spiritual nature, must be carried out not only with words and deeds, but no less with prayer and suffering.[60]

In a similar manner, there will come a day when we know it is time to take our leave. Like the former pope, we may feel physically tired and be ready to quit. Moses did. He cried out to God, saying that he was unable to carry and care for all of the people of Israel. Elijah cried out in the same way,

---

[60] http://edition.cnn.com/2013/02/11/world/pope-benedict-declaration/index.html?hpt=hp_t1

even to the point of wanting to die. Jonah was weary, sitting under a wilting vine in Nineveh. Even Paul was tired and ready to quit. The Lord appeared to him in a vision, telling him to keep on speaking and not to give up. There will be times in our lives when we will want to call it quits and make an exit, but many of us do not leave and we have to be shown the door.

For a variety of reasons, aging senior ministers struggle with leaving. One excuse after another is given as to why it is not time to retire. It is all the more difficult for individuals who launched the church or parachurch ministry to leave. Under their leadership, the ministry grew in size and influence. It is still 'their baby' in their thinking, and they struggle with handing 'their baby' over to another individual. All too often, the hesitancy with leaving can have something to do with power. George Barna cites Baby Boomers holding on to power as a primary reason why churches fail to pursue succession planning.

> "We love power. Whether it is because of an unhealthy desire for control, a reasonable concern about maintaining quality, a sense of exhilaration received from making pressure-packed, life-changing decisions or due to other motivations, Boomers revel in power. The sad result is that most Boomers—even those in the pastorate or in voluntary, lay-leadership positions in churches—have no intention of lovingly handing the baton to Baby Boomers."[61]

[61] http://www.barna.org Barna, George *Perspectives* "Gracefully Passing the Baton," 4/26/04.

Leaving a high level leadership position is unsettling for us. When retiring, we leave behind a significant piece of our self-worth and identity that has been rooted in our everyday work. Regretfully, we tend to stay too long in our role as the senior leader. Tens of thousands of pastors were reminded of this fact by Bill Hybels, founding pastor of Willow Creek Community Church. While speaking for the Leadership Summit in 2012, Hybels spoke of his transition into retirement. Moreover, he exhorted pastors with this reality.

> "Some of you attempt to hang on too long. Do the right thing for your church. When you get to your late 50s and on to your 60s make sure that your greatest legacy is going to be to make sure that your church is well led after you leave it."[62]

Push pause.
How weary are you? Be honest. What keeps you from thinking about retiring? Be honest. Will you have to be shown the door? If so, why?

TWO REASONS WHY WE STAY TOO LONG

Hybels and Willow Creek Community Church are in a four-phase succession plan, and Hybels speaks more openly about this season of life than he has in the past. He was interviewed by the Willow Creek Association for a Defining Moments presentation called "Your Church's Next Leader,"

---

[62] http://www.christianpost.com/news/bill-hybels-shares-succession-plans-at-leadership-summit-79787/

and during the interview, Hybels cited two primary reasons why senior ministers "hang on too long." Aging pastors put off retiring because 1) they lack sufficient retirement income, and 2) they lack an identity in retirement.

All too often, the soon-to-retire pastor has inadequate financial resources for retirement. Either the local church has failed to compensate him appropriately, providing him with a reasonable retirement package; or the pastor has been financially irresponsible by failing to set aside funds for his retirement years. Sometimes, both parties are at fault. Having insufficient funds for retirement is only made worse by the recent Great Recession of 2008. Many baby boomers have to delay their retirements because of a significant loss of wealth in their retirement accounts, and aging pastors are numbered among them. Boomers are enjoying improved physical health and enjoy longer life spans, so it should not surprise us that they are determined to work long past the typical retirement age. If this happens with a senior minister, it can cause great harm to the local church or ministry organization.

In the corporate world, a golden parachute is given to a retiring CEO. The individual receives a retirement bonus similar to a signing bonus of a star athlete. Seven and eight-figure retirement packages may happen in the business sector, but the same does not happen in the local church or parachurch organization. Mega-bonuses upon retirement are not common in the local church. Granted, a congregation will often times collect a love offering for the retiring pastor, but it is hardly sufficient to financially sustain him over the years ahead. In 1 Timothy 5:17-18, the Apostle Paul wrote of double honor being given to the Elders who direct the affairs of the church, particularly those whose ministry is that of preaching and teaching. Adequate compensation is but one way to provide appropriate honor. Though this is a sensitive subject, someone must lead the way and work with the retiring pastor to determine if he has sufficient resources for retirement. If he has little or no income for retirement, he will sense the need to continue serving in order to put food on his table and to keep a roof over his head. Church leaders must address this issue. Provide financial counseling for the retiring pastor; counseling that calculates anticipated living expenses during his retirement years and an estimated revenue stream to meet those expenses.

Similarly, Hybels believes that a senior minister stays too long because he has no post-ministry identity. When a pastor's complete identity is wrapped up in his life long ministry, he struggles with knowing what to do in an active retirement. After a fond farewell on his final Sunday, the retired pastor wakes up Monday morning wondering what to do and where to go.[63]

Our plight is similar to that of retired athletes. World class athletes struggle when they retire from their beloved sport. They are no longer in the spotlight. The cheering crowds have left. Accolades from the media are no longer given. Their fame no longer exists. In "The Woe After the Show," Max Linsky gathered the stories of many professional athletes who had no new identity when they went into retirement. Little thought is given by professional athletes as to what they will do when they walk away from the limelight.

---

[63] Bill Hybels. "Your Church's Next Leader," Defining Moments #1304, Barrington, IL: Willow Creek Association.

Statistics indicate that only five years into their retirement, sixty percent of NBA players "have nothing left," while in the NFL, nearly eighty percent of the players have nothing left from their earnings "after just two years."[64]

Far too many retirement stories of pastors sound similar to those of retiring athletes. When we fail to plan for life-after-the-ministry, we plan to fail. How were we able to lead the local church for decades when it seems that we cannot sufficiently lead ourselves in a time of expected transition? Even Plato was known to teach that the first and best victory is to conquer self. After spending years leading the church or parachurch organization through visionary seasons, we should have a vision for our own future, as well. If we have been capable of planning the future of the ministries we have led, we should be capable of planning our future.

Before retiring, it is essential to take the necessary time to prayerfully and strategically think what it is that God would want us to pursue in an active retirement. Provide counseling for the retiring pastor to aid in the development of a post-retirement identity. Betsy Kyte Newman, in her book *Retirement as a Career*, cites the transition into retirement as being pivotal.

> "The changes that retirement brings can either arrest our spiritual and psychological development or move us to new personal discoveries and a reintegration of ourselves. In retirement, we face ourselves without the burdens and distractions of work; if we stay with the

---

[64]http://www.slate.com/articles/sports/longform/2013/04/allen_iverson _terrell_owens_jose_canseco_sad_stories_about_retired_athletes.html

journey, and the fear and the pain it brings, we can discover a source of positive power, the path of our true purpose, and the real passion of our lives."[65]

Knowing that this transition could actually "move us to new personal discoveries," consider taking a lengthy sabbatical to focus on this crucial issue. The Elders and staff of The Creek provided me with a sabbatical, and while away from the daily responsibilities of ministry, I was able to seek God and His plan for what I refer to as 'life after The Creek.' During my sabbatical, I had a number of people praying for me; and when I returned, I was able to thank them because God did immeasurably more than all they could imagine or ask in prayer on my behalf. When I submitted a sabbatical accountability report to the Elders, it included the vision statement, mission statement and four rank-ordered core values of a ministry I hope to develop the day after I retire from The Creek. My post-retirement identity breathes life into me, and I am anxious to begin pursuing this God-honoring initiative.

Nowhere in all of Scripture do we find evidence of what we would describe as a western world model of retirement. An old saying declares, "If I'm not dead, I'm not done." Clearly, that is the sentiment and principle found in the Word. Though there comes a time when we will no longer serve as the lead servant in our ministry organization, we will still possess spiritual gifts and skills as a part of our leadership and pastoral nature that must be used while we are mentally and physically

---

[65] Betsy Kyte Newman, *Retirement as a Career* (Santa Barbara, CA: Praeger Publishers, 2008), p. 154.

capable. So then, dream. Go away to a quiet, secluded place where you can think carefully – and where you can hear God clearly. Ask and answer such questions as: What would I do if I were not serving as the leader of this ministry? What would I enjoy doing during the next five to ten years to advance the kingdom of God? Like Isaiah, if God calls me to serve Him in a unique way, will I say, "Here I am. Send me!"? While serving the Lord in other ways and elsewhere, how can I champion the work of my successor and church family so that only Jesus Christ is the Famous One? And while you are thinking, remember that God works through people who do not have to be important.

Christian theologian and preacher John Wesley (1703-91) modeled a life time of serving God for us. Wesley nearly died in a burning building as a child, but having been rescued from the flames, he devoted his life to serving God. In his eighty-seven years of life, John Wesley preached an estimated forty thousand sermons, wrote four hundred books, traveled roughly two hundred fifty thousand miles on horseback and learned to use ten languages in his study and writing. When he was eighty-three years old, Wesley complained that he could only write for fifteen hours a day because of his failing eye sight. At the age of eighty-six, he was humiliated in that he could only preach two sermons a day; and in his journal, Wesley candidly admitted that he struggled with lying in bed until five-thirty in the morning.[66] John Wesley had an active retirement—and so can we.

---

[66] http://www.denisonforum.org/cultural-commentary/696

Push pause.
How have you planned financially for your retirement? How has the church provided for your financial needs after retiring? Is this subject too sensitive to discuss with others? Why? What do you hope to do following retirement? How has your ministry identity developed past that of being the minister of the church you serve?

PASTOR EMERITUS

Some congregations will designate their retired minister as pastor emeritus. When they do so, it may be a designation in name only. After retiring, he will not have ministry responsibilities, nor will he receive an income for this role. It is merely a title given to honor the individual, as he chooses to stay active in the church that he faithfully and effectively served. However, when a long tenured pastor struggles with retiring because of a lack of planned income or identity, some congregations attempt to solve the dilemma by creating a post-retirement role of pastor emeritus. The emeritus designation is common in our culture, such as dean emeritus of the graduate school, etc. Emeritus status indicates that the individual has retired from active professional service, but has retained the title of his office or position. In the local church, the retiring pastor can become pastor emeritus; having more than an honorary position, but actually participating in ministry. Should the Leadership Continuity Team consider this option, it is important to clearly state—from the beginning—that the exiting leader has abdicated his leadership authority. In this way, the exiting leader does indeed exit. He leaves his position.

If the LCT retains the retiring pastor because he has limited financial resources for the years ahead, the salary and benefits must be carefully determined. Some congregations have actually made such generous retirement provisions that it negatively impacts the church budget, having allocated an excessive amount of resources to the pastor emeritus in his active retirement years. Leaders need to provide reasonable retirement benefits while the pastor is working, not after he leaves. Pay now – not later.

Some congregations also designate their retiring pastor as the emeritus in order to give him a post-retirement identity. If he has struggled to find a role outside of the local church, this designation helps solve his identity crisis. To that end, pastor emeritus status must have clearly defined roles and responsibilities within the church. It is essential that the pastor emeritus not serve in a leadership capacity, such as an elder or on the staff with positional authority. If the pastor emeritus is leading with authority in some manner, there is a risk of him diminishing the authority of his successor. A pastor emeritus can be helpful in providing pastoral care by making hospital calls, making visits to those who are shut-in, drawing alongside those grieving, etc. Moreover, a pastor emeritus can assist with fundraising. Should the church be in the process of building new facilities, doing capital improvements, or raising a significant amount of funds for a special initiative, a retired long tenured pastor can be of unique help. His former track record and continuing integrity can help foster generosity among the people.

In either situation, it is essential for the exiting leader to leave for an extended period of time, allowing and enabling his successor to transition into a position of leadership authority. Asking a retiring pastor to leave for at least a year is not out of the question. A lengthy, planned absence can actually help in bringing about an effective leader><shift because both the exiting and incoming leaders can focus intently on their new identities, while allowing the congregation to become well acquainted with their new senior pastor.

Following an unexpected health crisis, pastor and author Max Lucado left his position as senior minister of Oak Hills Church in San Antonio, Texas. With Randy Frazee now serving as the congregation's senior minister, Lucado remained on staff in the role of preaching minister. For individuals who choose to remain as a member of the church after retiring, Lucado offers the following three pieces of advice. First, the exiting leader must endorse his successor. There must not be the slightest hint of anything less in sentiment and attitude towards the new leader. Secondly, the exiting leader must release control to his successor, formally and genuinely. Moving off campus and leaving the church for an extended period of time aids in the transfer of control. Finally, the retired minister must find a new ministry outlet. Once the retired pastor adjusts to his new routine and is rested, he may want to preach and teach once again. While remaining as a member of the church, he can find new venues to serve God. Area churches will need interim pastors. Parachurch organizations in the area will need volunteer leaders.[67]

---

[67] Webinar on Succession Planning, featuring Max Lucado, Leadership Network, 3/26/13.

It is entirely possibly for the exiting leader to remain as a part of the congregation, whether in the role of pastor emeritus or as a lay member of the church. However, he must exit from his leadership position. He must abdicate his authority. When moving in this direction, do so prayerfully and with candid conversation. Responsibilities of the retired minister must be clearly stated and understood by all parties. There is no room for assumptions, as they often lead to misunderstanding and hard feelings. When a long tenured minister and his wife have invested their lives in the local church, they may choose to spend their autumn years with the people they have served and loved. It is entirely possible for a healthy friendship to exist between the exiting and incoming leaders, enabling the retired pastor and his wife to remain as a part of the church body; and when such a plan becomes reality, God is honored.

LEADERSHIP STYLES WHEN IN A LEADER><SHIFT

Phil Cooke is a Christian media consultant and producer, whose clients have included Billy Graham, Oral Roberts, Joel Osteen and a host of other communicators. He believes that Christian media is in the midst of one of the greatest generational transitions in the history of this industry. Moreover, Cooke is of the opinion that many transitions hit the wall and fail because the people involved give little or no consideration to the difference between leadership styles of first generation and second generation leaders.

First generation leaders are often the founders of ministries. They planted the church that then flourished under their leadership. It is common for first generation leaders to be driven, working relentlessly to launch the new ministry.

161

Ministry organizations and churches, in their early years, require tireless efforts to develop and sustain momentum. Working with creative energy, first generation leaders often lead alone. They have people assisting them, but not leading with them. First generation leaders tend to be the visionaries. Having charismatic personalities, they often do not work well in a team environment.

Second generation leaders are different. They lead teams of people and they value consensus. These leaders foster a team environment by inviting people to provide insights and ideas. Instead of leaning heavily on creativity, these individuals lean heavily on technology. Being less driven, second generation leaders pursue healthier relationships, particularly with family and close friends. When a leader><shift is in process, both leaders must be aware of these differences in style. If transitioning leaders do not recognize these variations, the succession plan can derail, particularly when leadership teams collide.

A first generation leader is surrounded by people who specialize at making things happen. They execute the vision and plan of their leader, specializing at making things happen. In contrast, a second generation leader is surrounded by people who have been given permission to help dream, and not merely work to make the dream come true. If a second generation leader inherits a team of older individuals who served his predecessor, the older team will struggle with being participatory and even think that their new leader is incompetent in comparison to their strong-handed and now retired leader. Stressful relationships result and anxiety levels rise because of possible staff changes because the younger

162

second generation leader may want to surround himself with new team members who replace existing staff members.[68]

To make a leadership transition work, it is essential for the exiting first generation leader to morph into a second generation leader. Yet, we who are older find it difficult to retool and reshape our leadership style into one that attracts and works well with younger people. Rather than assert our authority over the younger incoming leader, we should work alongside our successor and provide him with authority to begin leading. In a healthy leader><shift, one must intentionally become more while another intentionally becomes less.

If first generation leaders do not retool their leadership style into one that is conducive to making an effective transition, they may kill what could be a strong finish. Ed Stetzer, president of LifeWay Research and LifeWay's missiologist in residence, asks:

> "Why do some leaders end so well—Calvin Miller, Jack Hayford, Bob Russell, Roy Fish and so many more— while others go out not in a blaze of glory, but in a blaze of gory? They finish poorly and leave a mess in their wake. In some cases, they even undo some of the tremendous progress God used them to create in the years prior."[69]

---

[68] http://www.churchleaders.com/pastors/videos-for-pastors/164597-phil-cooke-making-leadership-transition-work.html
[69] http://www.churchleaders.com/pastors/pastor-blogs/165293-5-reasons-some-leaders-finish-poorly.html

After pondering the list of leaders who finished poorly, Stetzer identified five common factors among them. First, exiting leaders did not trust their successors. Those not finishing well were not satisfied with their successors, and in some instances, even sought new successors to replace the individuals originally selected. Second, leaders not finishing well argued over unimportant issues. They fought over matters that were of little or no consequence, particularly with regard to the successor. Third, leaders leaving poorly tried to control everything until their parting day. These individuals could not perceive someone else in the driver's seat, fearing that the individual would lead the ministry in a different manner or direction. Fourth, Stetzer noted that every leader who failed to finish well became increasingly angry; "their tone became louder, angrier and more belligerent. Openly blurting complaints was common."[70] Finally, even though these leaders were empowered by God to create and develop significant ministries, they could not hand over leadership to someone else.[71] Remember, succession planning is about more than the personality of a beloved leader. There is more at stake in these moments than a person's retirement. For the greater good of the church or ministry, an unhealthy exit must be firmly and compassionately circumvented by the larger leadership team (i.e., Elders, executive staff, etc.).

---

[70] Ibid.
[71] Ibid.

Push pause.

If the long tenured leader appears to be leaving poorly, how can the LCT intervene? If the exiting leader is incapable of retooling to a new leader-ship style that welcomes the next generation by both attitude and action, what should leaders of the church do in response?

LEAVING BEHIND A LEGACY

As a boy growing up, I vividly remember two assassinations of national leaders: President John F. Kennedy and the Reverend Martin Luther King, Jr. Like most people, I can tell you where I was standing and what I was doing when I first heard the news of these killings. But, it was not until many years later, that I understood something far more significant about these senseless murders. Both victims were young. Kennedy was only forty-six years old when he was killed, and Martin Luther King, Jr. was only thirty-nine. During their brief lives, both leaders impacted our culture in significant ways. That fact speaks volumes. What we learn from this observation is this: it matters not how long we live, but how we live. It is not the length of our lives that makes all the difference, but the depth of our lives. It is about legacy.

All of us have an opportunity to leave behind a legacy that is God honoring and kingdom advancing. Adoniram Judson, a missionary from the United States, served for thirty-eight years in Burma from 1812 until he died there in 1850. While serving in Burma, Judson suffered greatly: he was tortured and imprisoned in chains. His wife, Ann, died while in Burma, plunging Judson into a profound and long-lasting depression. Still, with his strength and faith anchored in God, he rebounded and he translated and published the New Testament for the Burmese people. By 1834, he accomplished the same with the Old Testament.

It is estimated that when Adoniram Judson died, there were a mere twelve to twenty-five professing Christians in all of Burma, and there were no established churches. Yet, at the 150th anniversary of the translation of the Bible into the Burmese language, the Burmese people were celebrating the work of Judson and noted the small print in the front of a Bible, stating: "Translated by Rev. A. Judson." Though there were only a handful of Christians at the time of his death, there are in excess of six hundred thousand Christians in Burma today, and all of them trace their spiritual heritage to one individual— Adoniram Judson. Though he never saw the fruit of his ministry with his own eyes, Judson left behind a spiritual legacy that will impact the eternity of countless people. [72]

We can and should leave behind a legacy—and of a particular kind. Christian author and speaker, John Maxwell, often challenges leaders to pursue the law of legacy. In his book *The 21 Irrefutable Laws of Leadership* (Thomas Nelson, 1998 & 2007), Maxwell writes that a leader's lasting value is measured by succession, and the law of legacy is one that the church should seek to follow.

Maxwell cites Coca-Cola for creating an environment that honors the law of legacy. In 1923, thirty-three year old Robert Woodruff was named president of Coca-Cola, a fledging soft drink company. Leading the company for five

---

[72] Julia Cameron, editor. *Christ Our Reconciler* (Downers Grove, IL: InterVarsity Press, 2012), pp. 200-201.

decades, Woodruff did much to turn the soft drink business into a giant company, particularly by developing a worldwide distribution system. It was Woodruff's goal to put a bottle of Coca-Cola in the hands of any soldier serving in any corner of the world during World War II. His visionary leadership moved the company forward by leaps and bounds.

Enter Roberto Goizueta. Born in Cuba and educated at Yale, Goizueta answered an ad for a bilingual chemist. He was hired at Coca-Cola, where he began to climb through the ranks of management, and he was noticed by Robert Woodruff. In the 1970s, Woodruff took Goizueta under wing and began mentoring him. Investing heavily in his young protégé, Woodruff named Roberto Goizueta the president and CEO of Coca-Cola in 1981. Under his leadership, Coca-Cola's market value increased from $4 billion to over $150 billion – an increase of more than 3,500 percent; making Coca-Cola the second most valuable company in America at the time. At the height of his leadership of the venerable company, Goizueta delivered a speech to the Executives' Club of Chicago, and in it, he said:

> "A billion hours ago, human life appeared on Earth. A billion minutes ago, Christianity emerged. A billion seconds ago, the Beatles performed on 'The Ed Sullivan Show.' A billion Coca-Colas ago...was yesterday morning."[73]

---

[73] John C. Maxwell, *Stewardship Strategies*; "The Law of Legacy: A Leader's Value is Measured by Succession" (Suwanee, GA: Injoy Stewardship Services, Spring 2006), pp. 1-3.

In less than a year after making this speech, Goizueta died. Struggling with cancer, he lived only six weeks following his diagnosis. Yet, Coca-Cola did not flounder. When news of his death became known, the company's market value did not plunge into a free fall. But rather, Goizueta had prepared for this moment in the same way that he had been prepared. Years previously, he had taken Douglas Ivester under wing and prepared him for this role. Goizueta continued practicing and pursuing the law of legacy by preparing a gifted successor who would have the skills and abilities to take the company further than he had done. This legacy demands that the current leader make the company as healthy and strong as possible, while preparing a successor who would have the capability to out-perform his mentor. Such companies are rare.[74] Such churches are rare.

Maxwell believes that leaders of all organizations can leave a legacy of effective succession by leading with a long view, meaning that they lead with the tomorrows of life in mind, not only with today in mind. As well, those leaving a legacy will create a culture of leadership, developing strong leaders at every level within the organization. This will require the organization to pay the price for developing leaders, realizing that an investment must be made in the present if there is to be a harvest of leaders in the future. Leaders leaving a legacy will value team leadership over and above individual leadership. A legacy driven leader values the entire team of leaders and admits that he alone cannot lead. Finally, a leader leaving behind a legacy of successful succession will walk

---

[74] Ibid.

away from the organization with absolute integrity. Maxwell writes:

> "Of all the laws of leadership, the Law of Legacy is the one that the fewest leaders seem to learn. Achievement comes to someone when he is able to do great things *for* himself. Success comes when he empowers followers to do great things *with* him. Significance comes when he develops leaders to do great things *for* him. But a legacy is created only when a person puts his organization into the position to do great things *without* him."[75]

Woodruff had Goizueta. Goizueta had Ivester. Moses had Joshua, and Elijah had Elisha, while Paul had Timothy. Who do we have? Who are we mentoring and preparing to lead the church more effectively than we ever did? The law of legacy calls for an older leader to intentionally invest in the life of a younger leader for the express purpose of advancing the kingdom of God in ways the exiting leader only dreamed of doing. A transformational leader inspires others to lead by investing in them: equipping and empowering them to lead. Have we created a leadership culture, one in which leaders are being developed throughout the ministry organization? If we are spending our time, resources and energy pursuing initiatives other than developing leaders, we will not finish strong—and we will have regrets.

It was 1904 when William Borden graduated from a Chicago high school. Young William was an heir to the Borden Dairy estate, and was already a millionaire. To celebrate his

---

[75] Ibid.

graduation from high school, his parents gave him a trip that took him around the world. As William traveled throughout Europe, the Middle East and Asia, he became painfully aware of the suffering of others. Borden became so emotionally burdened that he wrote to his parents, saying, "I'm going to give my life to prepare for the mission field." At this defining moment in this young man's life, he wrote two words in the back of his Bible: "No reserves."

Borden lived up to those two words as he held nothing back. While attending college at Yale University, Borden became a leader in the Christian community. During his first semester in college, Borden started a small prayer group that grew into a movement on campus, drawing one hundred-fifty freshmen together for Bible study and prayer every week. By the time Bill Borden was a senior, a thousand of Yale's thirteen hundred students were meeting in such groups on campus. Borden strategically made certain that students heard the good news of Christ while attending Yale, and he set an example of servant-leadership by reaching out to impoverished people living in New Haven, Connecticut. By graduation from college, the wealthy Borden committed himself to serving among the Muslims living in China. Graduation from Yale was another defining moment in his life, and once again he wrote two words in the back of his Bible. Alongside the words "no reserves," Borden wrote "no retreats."

Borden authentically lived that sentiment. Refusing a number of lucrative job offers, he went to graduate school, and after graduating from seminary, Borden went to Egypt to learn Arabic, as he intended to work among the Muslim Kansu people of China. While in Egypt, he contracted spinal meningitis. Within a month, twenty-five year-old William Borden was dead. Prior to dying, William Borden had written two more words in his Bible. Alongside the words "No reserves" and "No retreats," Borden wrote: "No regrets."[76] Will we write the same?

Push pause.
Will we leave behind a legacy? If so, describe that legacy? If not, why not? Moses had Joshua, and Elijah had Elisha, while Paul had Timothy. Who do we have? Who are we mentoring and preparing to lead the church more effectively than we ever did? How can we develop a deep bench now?

---

[76] www.preachingtoday.com citing Bill White, Paramount, California; sources: *Daily Bread* (12-31-1988); *The Yale Standard* (Fall 1970); Mrs. Howard Taylor, Borden of Yale (Bethany House, 1988).

Reality #13:
The Incoming Leader Leads

*So the LORD said to Moses, "Take Joshua son of Nun, a man in whom
is the spirit of leadership, and lay your hand on him. Have him stand
before Eleazar the priest and the entire assembly and commission him
in their presence. Give him some of your authority so the whole
Israelite community will obey him.*
Numbers 27:18-20

Moses became less while Joshua became more. A
leader>\<shift happened between them and it was witnessed by
millions of people in route to the Promised Land. Moses had
just prayed: "May the LORD, the God who gives breath to all
living things, appoint someone over this community to go out
and come in before them, one who will lead them out and bring
them in, so the LORD's people will not be like sheep without a
shepherd" (Numbers 27:16-17). God answered the prayer of
Moses by providing Joshua, and Joshua had to hit the ground
running. As the new, incoming leader (IL), Joshua had to lead.
The people were not looking for a motivational speaker, they
were looking for a leader who would take them to the
Promised Land.

Many churches today are not looking for a leader; so
much as they are looking for a performer. Think of it this way.
While writing this chapter, the NFL season officially began last
evening and like many guys, I was glued to the television. I
happened to be watching Peyton Manning make NFL history,
becoming only the sixth quarterback in NFL history to throw

seven touchdown passes in a single game. My interest in watching Manning is because he is no longer playing for our beloved Indianapolis Colts. After a year on the sidelines while recuperating from surgery, Peyton Manning left the Colts for the Denver Broncos, where he hit the ground running. An NFL team has fifty-three players, but the team's rise and fall hinges on one player—the quarterback. If he can throw the ball and connect with receivers downfield, they can score, much to the approval of the fans.

The same happens on a Sunday morning. Time and again, people will sit in church and expect the preacher to connect with them. Regretfully, far too many people have the mindset of a fan in that they want a performer, someone who can preach effectively just as a quarterback throws the ball effectively. Attendance and offering rise and fall based on the preacher's ability to perform on Sunday morning because of the consumer-minded people in the church. Yet, just as a quarterback is surrounded by fifty-two capable and necessary players, the preacher is surrounded by others on the leadership team—and they want to be led. Even though people do not always admit it, deep down they want to be led. When Jesus saw the crowds, He was overwhelmed with compassion for them as they were "harassed and helpless like sheep without a shepherd" (Matthew 9:36). People in the time of Christ wanted a leader and nothing has changed since then. People want to be led. Not only do we need the successor to communicate the Word of God creatively and effectively, but we need him to lead. The incoming leader (IL) must lead.

As mentioned in the first chapter of this book, the American Church is facing days of unprecedented demand and high capacity leaders are needed now more than ever before. Where do we find them? How will we recognize them? What should we look for in a likely candidate? These questions — and more — can vex us. Knowing that we need more than a performer and agreeing that we need a leader, we will explore the multifaceted issues of the incoming leader by using the interrogatives of speech. Do you remember using and asking these questions: who, what, why, when, where and how? Interrogatives are investigative, and they help us understand some of the unique issues involving the successor. The following issues are not exhaustive and all-inclusive. But rather, the following items help to stir our thinking when it comes to the incoming leader.

WHY

Previously, in chapter 4, we were reminded of how important it is to start with the why. So then, why is the incoming leader such a significant issue when it comes to succession planning? Simply put, the most expensive hire is the wrong hire. A church or parachurch ministry cannot invest too much time, energy or resources to make certain that the incoming leader is the right leader for the ministry.

It was a cold January day when a young, forty-three year-old man became the leader of his nation. At his inauguration, a renowned general of their nation was standing beside him, who had commanded their country's armies in a war that resulted in the defeat of Germany just fifteen years previously. The new, young leader was raised as a Roman Catholic. The nation celebrated their newly appointed leader with parades and parties that lasted into the early hours of the morning. Who was the incoming leader? Adolf Hitler. Were you assuming it was John F. Kennedy? If so, you were missing one important piece of information, and that being the date of the inaugural--January 30, 1933.[77]

The above illustration serves as an example of how we make assumptions based on incomplete information. We can jump to the conclusion that we have the right successor selected when in fact; we have made that decision based on incomplete information. When a leader><shift is about to happen, it is vitally important that we have completed our due diligence in thoroughly vetting the candidate. Why? As stated above, the most expensive hire is a wrong hire. Why we must make the right successor selection is trumpeted by Chand and Bronner in their book: *Planning Your Succession*.

> "Our organizations need to experience a profound change in focus about succession planning. We must make the critical connection between organizational success and leadership sustainability...acquiring and retaining the right leaders has become every bit as vital as having the right business strategy."[78]

Getting the right person at the right time, using his right gifts for the right reason and with the right attitude will bring about the success in succession for which we pray and

---

[77] Simon Sinek. *Start With Why: How Great Leaders Inspire Everyone to Take Action* (New York: The Penguin Group, 2009), p. 11.

[78] Samuel R. Chand and Dale C. Bronner *Planning Your Succession: Preparing for the Future* (Highland Park, IL: Mall Publishing Co., 2008), p. 52.

hope. This first interrogative peals back the outer layer of our investigation to reveal the next obvious question.

WHAT

The LCT must determine what the church or parachurch organization is looking for in a candidate. Regretfully, many people – whether on the LCT or sitting in the pew—want a successor who is just like his predecessor in every way. The incoming leader cannot be a clone of the exiting leader. Though they should have some similarities, there should also be some differences. For example, the incoming leader may have different communication and leadership styles, as well as a different personality temperament. As well, the incoming leader may have different ideas and methods for leading the staff team, while pursuing the stated vision of the church or ministry. Recognize that some differences are needed and should be expected.

When compiling a written candidate profile for what you are looking for in the successor, I urge you to begin with values. Particularly, there should be two values that rise to the top of the candidate description just as cream rises to the top of milk, and these two values are a direct reflection of the two greatest commandments: we are to love God and love people (Mark 12:30-31). The two most important values in a potential successor are his spiritual values and the value he places upon people. His spiritual vitality is of supreme importance. A candidate can have exemplary academic credentials and a sterling ministry record, but if he does not love God with all of his heart, mind, soul and strength; he will not be an ideal candidate. Moreover, he must have a sincere love for people, both inside and outside of the body of Christ. God loves people. They matter greatly to Him, and people must be highly valued by the successor. When giving consideration to the individual's ability to preach, teach and lead at exceptional levels; remember to give careful thought as to what depth he loves God and people.

When developing the successor profile, you will need to address at least three categories of concern: 1) spiritual vitality, 2) professional ability, and 3) personal stability. As previously stated, the successor's spiritual values are of the greatest concern. No matter what our culture says, character counts in a leader. In this section of the profile, list items that would be indicators of his walk with God; in terms of his past, present and future journey. Joshua was an ideal successor to Moses because he had a solid spiritual formation. Elisha was a model successor to Elijah as he was filled with a double portion of his mentor's spirit. In much the same manner, the incoming leader must have a solid spiritual formation, while yielding to the control of the indwelling Holy Spirit. Regarding his professional ability, list what educational credentials you require, as well as experiential requirements from previous ministry positions. Describe practical ministry skills that the successor is expected to have. Finally, intentionally explore the personal dimensions of his life: marriage, family and finances would be appropriate places with which to begin. The profile must address this aspect of life because he will be setting an example for the people by the life with which he lives.

As you review resumes and references, keep in mind that there are intangible qualities not visible on paper (i.e., attitudes, people skills, emotional intelligence, etc.). To assess his intangible traits, create opportunities to watch the candidate in action. If your successor is an internal candidate, you will have ample opportunities for observing these qualities in his day-to-day ministry. If the candidate is external, you will have to design some extended times for the candidate to engage your staff, your leadership team, and your congregation, while you observe these qualities.

Moreover, as you describe the ideal successor on the profile, remember to include his need to lead. If your church or ministry practices strategic planning, describe where you believe God can and will take your organization in the next three to five years—or longer, and then determine if the candidate successor has the skills necessary to lead the church or ministry to this place of preferred future. Again, it is important that the candidate willingly embrace the vision, mission and core values of the church as they have already been developed by those currently leading the ministry. Then again, if the ministry has no sense of vision or direction, your candidate profile will need to state that you are looking for a successor who can help facilitate, pursue and accomplish a God-honoring vision.

The list of what the candidate should resemble can go on and on, but I deliberately end with this character trait; the candidate must possess authentic humility, and this is easy to detect. John Dickson, author of *Humilitas*, spots humility in the life of the late Sir Edmund Hillary (1919-2008), the first man to summit Mt. Everest, along with this friend and guide, Tenzin Norgay. Following this great achievement, Hillary was knighted by the Queen Elizabeth II of England. That

178

recognition was followed by a number of notable achievements. Sir Hillary was appointed New Zealand's highest commissioner to India, Nepal, and Bangladesh; and he later was awarded Britain's highest civilian award, the Order of the Gater. Throughout his lifetime of achievement, Sir Hillary maintained and modeled a life marked with authentic humility. Dickson described a moment when Hillary's true humility was most conspicuous.

> "On one of his many trips back to the Himalayas he was spotted by a group of tourist climbers. They begged for a photo with the great man, and Hillary obliged. They handed him an ice pick so he would look the part and set up for the photograph. Just then another climber passed the group and, not recognizing the man at the center, strode up to Hillary saying, 'Excuse me, that's not how you hold an ice pick. Let me show you.'"[79]

The people with Sir Hillary watched in stunned silence while the legendary man thanked a fellow climber for his advice, adjusting the ice pick in his hands, and continuing with the photograph. This moment in Sir Edmund Hillary's life models a truth worth embracing, particularly when a leader><shift is about to occur, and that truth is this: God works through people who do not need to be important.

---

[79] John Dickson, *Humilitas* (Grand Rapids: Zondervan, 2011), pp. 70-71.

Push pause.
What does your written profile of the position include or not include? How can we discern if a leader feels the need to be important?

WHO

All of us have grown up with the world of Disney. Whether we watched the one-hour Disney show on Sunday evenings during the early years of television or we traveled to one of the Disney theme parks, our lives have been impacted by the thinking of the late Walt Disney. In the late 1960s, after the success of Disneyland in southern California, the venerable visioneer purchased forty-seven square miles of unattractive and unwanted swampland in central Florida. Disney's dream was to build an "experimental prototype community of tomorrow." He dubbed this dream EPCOT for short. His plan included building a city, featuring homes, hotels, factories, shopping centers, office complexes, school systems, church buildings, factories and more. Walt Disney wanted to build the world's finest model city as a response to the many problems cities were then facing.

But before his beloved project could be completed, Walt Disney died on December 15, 1966. Not only did Disney die that day, but his dream died with him. Those who led the company in his place did not know how to proceed with his vision. So they did what they already knew how to do; they built an amusement park. In 1971, the Magic Kingdom opened. Disney World became a larger and more grandiose version of Disneyland. Over the years, people complained to the management of Disney that they were unable to accomplish the vision of their founder. So, in the mid-1990s, Celebration, Florida, became a recognized incorporated municipality, developed by the Disney Company. The EPCOT we know of is another amusement park that opened in 1982, but the EPCOT of which Walt Disney dreamed did not become a community where people lived until three decades after his death. What happened at Disney happens in the church.

Who could be a likely successor candidate? Simply said, a person who is able to embrace the vision and carry it to fruition. If the church or ministry has a clearly stated vision and mission, the incoming leader must be willing and able to embrace the established strategic plan and move in that direction. If a person is hired to drive a bus for the city, he must have the ability to drive the bus, carrying people along an already established route. He cannot develop a new route all his own. Many transitions fail because a new leader decides that the current strategic plan or vision of the ministry is lacking, and only he is capable of casting a new and appropriate vision. Granted, if your church or ministry has no stated vision or direction; then by all means, recruit a successor who is capable of developing and implementing a God-honoring vision. Finding a successor capable of pursuing an established vision is critical to the continued forward momentum of the church during a leader><shift.

There is a second unique issue when it comes to asking who should be the successor. Should the son of the retiring minister be his successor? What do you think of hiring a son? Such a succession does occur. When Jerry Falwell died of an apparent heart attack while sitting at his desk in 2007, there was no succession plan in place for the megachurch he founded

181

and led. Today, the church is led by Falwell's son, Jonathan Falwell. The late John Osteen founded the Lakewood Church in Houston, Texas, and following his death in 1999, his son, Joel Osteen, was named as his successor. These are but two of the more nationally known and recognized successions between a father and son, and far more are occuring that are less known to us.

Should a son succeed his father as the pastor of the church or leader of a ministry? The above two examples certainly indicate that sons can lead in place of their fathers, providing momentum and leading so as to produce growth. Often times, when a son is his father's successor, he typically serves on the staff of the church prior to his appointment as the new leader. Case in point, Joel Osteen served on the staff of Lakewood Church for years while his father was the senior pastor. When family members are on the staff of the church or ministry organization, nepotism is practiced. Nepotism happens in the world of politics, business, entertainment, and even in the church. Nepotism shows favoritism to relatives by employing them, and sometimes they are hired regardless of their capabilities. It should not surprise us then that many organizations—including churches—have anti-nepotism policies. Moreover, some organizations welcome nepotism and have policies in place to accommodate the practice.

This is a most controversial subject, and people have agreed to disagree when it comes to this issue. Business executives hold to different positions regarding nepotism, as do politicians and pastors. If you are thinking of hiring the son of the pastor as a successor, please take into consideration that there will be some in the congregation who are of the opinion

182

that he is the successor only because of his last name; and it will be difficult to convince them otherwise. This will give birth to resentment, and not only among members of the church, but potentially among those individuals on the staff. There may be staff members who think they should have been given consideration to serve as the incoming leader, and when the son of the current leader is chosen, a spirit of bitterness will take root. As well, what if he does not fulfill the expectations that have been listed on the candidate profile? What if he falls short in a category or two? Some may be in favor of the senior minister's son becoming the next pastor of the church, but if he is unable to meet the position requirements and he is still named as the successor, he is destined for trouble. Not only will he come to dislike the ministry, but it is possible that he will resent those who helped put him in the position — including his father, the former pastor. It is essential that the son meet and even exceed the position profile requirements. Hiring a son is a sensitive issue, and it is one that requires extra care and caution. Succession is not about advancing any particular personality; but rather, it is about advancing the kingdom of God.

WHERE

Where to find the ideal candidate is one of the most often asked questions when it comes to succession; and the answer to that question is twofold. The candidate is either found internally or externally. Just as with the issue of nepotism, this concern is also controversial. There are individuals firmly of the opinion that the best candidates are always found within the church or ministry organization, while

183

there are others who believe that the candidate must come from the outside.

As Bill Hybels' retirement nears, Willow Creek favors appointing a successor from within the church. They are looking first for an internal candidate. In his interview with the Willow Creek Association on transitioning leaders, Hybels said that the church will observe staff members for at least for two years. Hybels would rather appoint someone from within the ranks, but he realizes that there may not be an individual capable of leading at this level. If a person is not found, then they will look externally. Specifically, they will try to find a person serving in a similar ministry environment and serving at an exceptional level. The candidate—whether internal or external—must be a high capacity leader because of the demands faced by leading at Willow. [80]

One obvious advantage in hiring an external candidate is that he brings a fresh set of eyes to the church or ministry organization. They have a new, objective perspective of what is currently taking place in the ministry; and if the church or organization is troubled and faltering, it should be of no surprise to us that many Leadership Continuation Teams look for an external candidate. Yet, be sure to take into consideration that there must be a match between the external candidate and the organizational culture. The church or ministry should have clearly stated faith statements, a vision statement, a mission statement and rank-ordered core values; and the external candidate must embrace these foundational elements that create an internal culture. A mismatch of the

---

[80] Bill Hybels, Defining Moments Interview #1304: "Your Church's Next Leader" Interview. Barrington, IL: Willow Creek Association.

external candidate with the internal culture can spell defeat for the succession. Cultural compatibility is essential if momentum is to be maintained while handing the baton to the next generation leader.

So then, one obvious advantage in hiring an internal candidate is that he is already well-established in the church and organizational culture. He knows of the past, present and future of the church, and is familiar with the traditions and values that are interwoven into the fabric of the church community. As a result, an external candidate is not the only individual capable of rescuing a troubled church or ministry organization. An internal candidate who has served on the staff of the church understands the culture and working of the organization, and can then serve as a powerful and potential agent of change. An internal candidate is a known factor to the constituents. He has a known ministry track record. His strengths and weaknesses are already known. His family is well-acquainted with the community of believers. These are just a short list of the many benefits of looking for a successor with in the church. Particularly, if we create a legacy of leaders as described in the previous chapter, we will have ample candidates within the church to first consider as successors. Still, there is a risk. Remember that a high capacity leader is not going to wait forever to be named as the successor. He may sense God leading him to a venue where his leadership skills can be put to use in advancing the kingdom of God more effectively; and being a faithful steward of his life, he may choose to move on down the road.

Push pause:
Where will you look for your successor? If you look externally, will you be contacting Christian universities, colleges and seminaries; ministry organizations and other churches? If you look internally, how will you approach the different people on the staff team? Can you consider more than one individual for the position? If so, how will you communicate with multiple candidates? In your setting, what direction appears to be more advantageous—seeking a candidate internally or externally?

HOW

Once we have a profile completed and we know what kind of candidate we are seeking, we may determine that an external search will be necessary. How do we find a high capacity leader? Are we capable of doing so?

It was the fall of 2010, and all eyes were on Chile. Millions of people from around the world were keeping watch around the clock to see if thirty-three miners, trapped more than two-thousand feet under solid rock, would survive. Their main tunnel had collapsed, and all the miners were doomed to die. There was little hope of survival. They were eating two spoons of tuna, taking a sip of milk and eating pieces of peaches every other day in hopes of surviving. For two months, they prayed and hoped that someone would save them. Engineers from around the world worked intensely to reach the men, and they did. On October 13, 2010, each and every miner was brought back to the surface. Raised in a thirteen foot long rescue capsule, the miners were rescued, one by one. When we think of their situation, it is obvious that they needed help, and it came from the outside. In much the same way, when looking for a successor, it may be that we need help in finding them, and the help comes from the outside.

How can we find a high capacity leader? A church or ministry organization can turn to helping professionals who specialize in this very task. For example, the Slingshot Group (www.slingshotgroup.org) is a team of individuals who work at connecting a church with an external candidate. Slingshot does extensive research of each candidate, and researches the hiring church or organization, as well. The Slingshot Group wants to aim people in the right direction, "slinging" them to a place of ministry opportunity that is a right match of an individual's gifts, skills, experience, and education with a church or ministry organization in need of a successor. The Slingshot Group works with literally hundreds of trained and experienced pastors, and they want to work alongside of you to locate the ideal external candidate. The Vanderbloemen Search Group provides similar services for the local church (www.vanderbloemen.com). This ministry group works with a church to develop both an emergency and long-term succession plan, as well as to assist in finding an external candidate successor.

When we call for help from the outside, we are not admitting defeat. Our source of networking may be limited, and the high capacity leader that we need is not going to be found through our traditional channels, like that of sending an e-mail to a distribution list of colleagues. Remember, the wrong hire is the most costly hire. If the successor is an external candidate, we need to throw the net wide, and getting help from the outside can be one of the best decisions we make in succession planning process. Proverbs 11:14 reminds us that "many advisors make victory sure." Be willing to seek the advice of many godly counselors.

Push pause.
For a variety of reasons, some churches hesitate to get help from outside agencies when looking for a new leader for the church. What is your take on this issue regarding the incoming leader? Have you attempted this in the past? Are you willing to do so in the future? If not, why not?

WHEN

Old Testament Daniel is an inspiration to many, and when we look deeply into his story—past the popular stories of the lion's den and the fiery furnace—we discover rich truth. One life impacting discovery for me came in the form of three simple words found in Daniel 4; the story of King Nebuchadnezzar being driven to live in the wild among the animals. The king had a dream, but it was more like a nightmare in that it troubled him. Daniel interpreted his nightmare:

"You will be driven away from people and will live with the wild animals; you will eat grass like the ox and be drenched with the dew of heaven. Seven times will pass by for you until you acknowledge that the Most High is sovereign over all kingdoms on earth and gives them to

anyone he wishes. The command to leave the stump of the tree with its roots means that your kingdom will be restored to you when you acknowledge that Heaven rules. Therefore, Your Majesty, be pleased to accept my advice: Renounce your sins by doing what is right, and your wickedness by being kind to the
oppressed. It may be that then your prosperity will continue."[81]

Daniel had already won the favor of King Nebuchadnezzar with his skill of interpreting dreams, and that is why the king summoned Daniel to help him understand this dream. Because of his pride and refusal to acknowledge God as the provider of all, King Nebuchadnezzar lost his throne, only to be driven into the wild to live among the animals. Now imagine the king's surprise when nothing happened to him. Kings were absolute rulers. Whatever they wanted, they received. Orders they gave were to be obeyed immediately and without hesitation. They must have looked at life through the lens of the instant: instant obedience, instant gratification, and instant response to their every whim. So, when Daniel prophesied that the king would be driven from the palace to live among the animals, I venture to think that he expected it to happen immediately. But, nothing happened. The next day, he woke up still living in the palace. Days turned into weeks, weeks into months, and even months passed into a year. The king was still living high and mighty until "twelve months later" (verses 28-29). Imagine that—an entire year passed before Daniel's interpretation of the dream became reality.

---

[81] Daniel 4:25-27.

With so much time passing by, the king may have thought that Daniel's interpretation was wrong. Yet, such thinking is far from wrong.

Those three simple words remind me that God has His own sense of timing and it is far different from our sense of timing. Throughout Scripture, we read of one event after another where God's unique timing was conspicuous. So it should be of no surprise to us that we must be both sensitive and surrendered to God's sense of timing with regard to the incoming leader. Be mindful as to when God prompts you to begin the search for a successor. Look for the prompting of God as to when to pass the baton of authority to the incoming leader, both partially and completely.

God told Moses to "give him (Joshua) some of your authority so the whole Israelite community will obey him" (Numbers 27:20). God determined when Eli no longer served as Israel's leader, but Samuel rose to that position. David respected the timing of God in a most serious and sincere way. Though he had ample opportunity to kill King Saul, David refused to do so. He waited for God's timing to elevate him to the throne. The mantle of leadership passed from Elijah to Elisha at a time of God's own choosing, and not a day earlier or later. These are but a few of the many scriptural examples indicating that God has His own sense of time. We must acknowledge and respect this truth.

The world renowned architect Frank Lloyd Wright once told of something that happened to him while he was a child that had a significant impact on him for the remainder of his life. When he was nine years of age, he walked across a snow covered field with his uncle; and this uncle had a serious sense of focus in life. When they reached the other side of the field, the uncle had his young nephew turn around to look at their tracks in the snow. The uncle emphasized how he had walked in a straight and direct path, while pointing out to nine-year old Frank that he had roamed all over the field in a variety of directions, "Notice how your tracks wander aimlessly from the fence to the cattle to the woods and back again," his uncle said. "And see how my tracks aim directly to my goal. There is an important lesson in that." The great architect enjoyed telling this story as it helped people understand his philosophy in life and work: "I determined right then," he said with a twinkle in his eye, "not to miss most things in life, as my uncle had."[82]

Too often, we are like Frank Lloyd Wright's uncle in that we are direct and permit no 'aimless wandering' in life. We are driven, having little or no margin in our lives to be still in the presence of God. We are driven and direct, we often miss what God is attempting to reveal to us. We do not permit Him to get our attention, to direct our paths, or to prompt our actions. It has not escaped me that when the magicians of Egypt's pharaoh could not imitate the miracles of Moses any longer, they turned to their king and declared, "This is the finger of God" (Exodus 8:19). Pagan magicians were able to recognize the hand of God that enabled Moses to perform miracles before their very eyes.

As believers, do we recognize God with and among us? Slow down. Listen well. Think deeply. Do not run ahead of God when it comes to finding and appointing a successor. Over and again, the phrase "wait for the Lord" appears in

---

[82] Barry L. Marrow and Kenneth Boa. *Yearning for More* (Downers Grove, IL: IVP Books, 2013), p. 106.

191

Scripture. "But I am still confident of this: I will see the goodness of the Lord in the land of the living. Wait on the Lord, be strong and take heart, and wait on the Lord" (Psalm 27:13-14). Wait means wait.

Reality #14:
Others Matter

Do nothing out of selfish ambition or vain conceit,
but in humility, consider others better than yourselves.
Each of you should look not only to your own interests,
but also to the interests of the others.
Philippians 2:3-4

Patti was a war demonstrator. In the early 1980s, she—along with many Americans—attended peace rallies and demanded an end to nuclear armament. Patti was a much sought-after speaker and was widely recognized across America because of her family ties. Patti Davis was the daughter of then-president Ronald Reagan. Time and again, Ronald Reagan attempted to talk with his daughter, but she refused to pursue conversation with him; and today, this is one of her great regrets. While being an anti-war activist, Davis admits that she was at war with her father. She spoke candidly in an interview about the relationship she shared with her father and admitted having regrets. During the interview, Davis referred to the time when her father struggled with Alzheimer's:

> "I would look into my father's eyes and try to reach past the murkiness of Alzheimer's with my words, my apology, hoping that in his heart he heard me and understood...I wish that now, all those years ago, I had led with kindness, not with ideological stridency. We

193

are, after all, remembered in the end for how we treat others. Sometimes the political has to be tempered by the personal."[83]

Patti Davis regrets their failed relationship. She readily admits that their father-daughter relationship could have been a much healthier had she made different choices. The same is true for us, particularly when a leader><shift is occurring. For a variety of reasons, we experience regrets from failed relationships between one another. This is true not only for the exiting and incoming leaders, but it is also true of those within the congregation or the parachurch organization's constituency. Many churches fail at their attempt to execute a succession plan because of the failure rate in relationships between the key players in the plan.

GETTING ALONG BEFORE MOVING ALONG

Did you learn to drive a manual transmission when you took driver's education? I did. Years ago, more people drove vehicles known to have a "stick shift." My first car was a Chevy Impala with "three on a tree"; meaning that the gear lever was on the right side of the steering column. Since learning to drive in the early 1970s, I have chosen to drive vehicles that have a manual transmission because I enjoy doing so. For many people, learning to drive a manual transmission is difficult. When I was first married, I tried teaching my young bride how to drive our Plymouth Horizon because it was a stick shift. It was very difficult for Leah, and after repeatedly stalling the engine while attempting to shift gears,

---

[83] Davis, Patti. "Saying No to Daddy," *Town & Country*, January, 2012.

she gave up. She was done and there was no trying to get her back behind the wheel.

To some people, learning to drive a succession plan is like learning to drive a manual transmission. It is difficult. After struggling to work through a succession planning process, some individuals give up. They quit because it is just too hard, particularly in trying to get along with one another throughout the process. This is particularly true of the exiting and incoming leaders. When the successor is working with his predecessor prior to the transition, they must pursue relational health. They both must get along before one of them moves along.

Kristin Scott Thomas, the British-born actress who was nominated for an Oscar for her role in *The English Patient* (1996), spoke in an interview of how growing older in a culture that adores youth causes pressure in life. The fifty-three year-old actress confided:

> "When you're my age, you're invariably in a supporting role, so there's often a young woman in her 20s or early 30s who is the lead, and you're constantly put next to them. You're watching yourself get old, on a screen that hides nothing. I'm not talking about in a private setting, at a dinner party or anything. But when you're walking down the street, you get bumped into, people slam doors in your face—they just don't notice you."[84]

---

[84] Sheryl Garratt, "Kristin Scott Thomas: Men Will Run When They See This" *The Telegraph*, August 5, 2013.

A cultural chasm exists between those who are older and those who are younger, thus creating more pressure between the retiring minister and his successor. This makes an authentic and healthy relationship between the exiting and incoming leaders all the more challenging and essential. From the comments made by Kristin Scott Thomas, one could speculate that she experiences inner monologues, sometimes referred to as one-sided conversations of the mind. Have you had such conversations? I certainly have, and they are a waste of time. When we struggle in key relationships it is far easier to have an inner monologue than to actually pursue candid, deeper conversation with a colleague in hopes of fostering a healthier, God-honoring relationship.

Most Americans shun deep conversation, choosing rather, to engage in what I call cliché conversation. Cliché conversation involves little more than an exchange of greetings between one another. Going a bit deeper in conversation, we begin to share facts with one another. Facts are indisputable, such as telling someone that it is raining outside, when in fact, it is. Going deeper still, we begin to share our opinions with others. This is the depth at which authentic communication begins. The moment we share our opinions, we open ourselves to the risk of being rejected by the person with whom we are speaking. Think about that. Who among us likes to be rejected? If we share our opinion about a sports team, a political bias, a spiritual belief or more; we can find ourselves friendless. So, to play it safe, most Americans do not venture into the realm of deeper conversation because they want to be liked and accepted by others. This is not only true about teenagers. Grown men and women fear being rejected, so they choose to wade in the waters of shallow conversation. What is truly needed, though, is an indomitable will and desire to go deep; to desire conversation that involves even the sharing of our emotions, while being completely candid and honest. If an older predecessor and a younger successor are struggling to get along, communication at this deepest level is essential for them to work together in hopes of transitioning effectively.

Push pause.
Describe your style and typical level of communication. What keeps you from going deeper in meaningful, helpful conversation? When you consider your leadership team, how well do you communicate? What would have to happen for effective communication to occur?

   Relational health can be enjoyed between transitioning leaders. We have seen such health modeled for us not only in a handful of successful transitions, but also in the Scriptures. One of the strongest relationships in the Bible between two transitioning leaders was that of Moses and Joshua. The Scriptures describe how Joshua was given some of the authority of Moses (Numbers 27:12-23), even though Moses still led the entire nation of Israel prior to his death. For example, after transferring a portion of his authority to Joshua, Moses then led the army of Israel into battle against the Midianites (Numbers 31:1f). Their leadership roles began to change. One became more while another became less. As time passed, there came a defining moment when Moses declared Joshua the leader of the Israelites and he was formally commissioned (Deuteronomy 31:1-8, 14-15). It was not long after this moment that Moses hiked high up Mt. Nebo and from that lofty vantage point, God showed to him the Promised Land. Moses then died and God buried him in Moab in an unmarked grave (Deuteronomy 34). Moses, the man who singlehandedly led a few million people out of slavery in Egypt and then wandered through a desert wasteland for forty years, was given no accolades and received no applause. Then again, he needed none. After all, Moses was known as the most humble person on the face of the earth (Numbers 12:3). God was more than enough for him, and the manner in which his life ended reflected his humility.

The humility of Moses played a major role in his relational health with Joshua. Moses was not threatened by this up and coming leader. He was not envious of his prayer time with God. Take a look at Exodus 33:7-11. It was the practice of Moses to pitch a Tent of Meeting in the Israelite camp, and he would go there to pray. He took Joshua along with him and taught him how to encounter God through prayer. It is interesting that after Moses finished praying, Joshua remained in the Tent of Meeting for a longer period of time. The mentoring that Moses provided Joshua was effective as the successor was furthered strengthened in his spiritual formation. Moses was not threatened by this development. To the contrary, he would have been greatly encouraged. Throughout the story of their relationship, it appears that one became less while another became more, which is a mark of relational health.

As we reflect on the healthy relationship that existed between Moses and Joshua, we should give serious consideration to imitating them, particularly when it comes to mentoring. If both the exiting and incoming leaders are authentically humble men of God, mentoring of the younger by the older is not only possible, but it will be welcomed. An intensive mentoring relationship can be developed between the two men, with stated expectations and objectives. The mentoring can happen casually as the younger pastor observes the older pastor lead, but there must be actual times of teaching, just as when Moses took Joshua into the Tent of Meeting and taught him how to meet with God. When the exiting and incoming leaders are working together on the same staff team, mentoring is essential; and fruitful mentoring will happen only when two men are humble.

Moses and Joshua provide another helpful insight for us. There came a defining moment when Moses told the Israelites that Joshua was their leader, and the same must happen in our transitions. Exiting leaders can help incoming leaders by doing the same. In our last staff meeting or worship service, we can say to those around us, "Today, I am your pastor and tomorrow I will not be your pastor." We not only declare the incoming leader the pastor of the church, but we also declare him to be our pastor. It is essential for us to sincerely declare the incoming leader your leader and mine, and that we will have his back. Just as we wanted people to pray for us, defend us and encourage us through the years, we must do the same for our successor. Publicly declare your successor to be your pastor. Encourage people to remain in contact with you as a friend, but not as their pastor. Let people know that if they e-mail or call you to express their concern about their new pastor that you will forward the e-mail or information directly to the new pastor on their behalf. Do not allow yourself to be pulled into divisive conversation about your successor. You must pursue relational health with your successor, working to get along after moving along.

Push pause.
How have you mentored future leaders in the past and how are you doing it in the present? In particular, describe your mentoring relationship with your successor or those who may become your successor someday.

WE ARE IN THIS TOGETHER

While relational health is needed between the exiting and incoming leaders, a spirit of unity is needed throughout the church or ministry organization in a time of succession. The church and parachurch organization are exceptionally vulnerable to the sly attacks of the evil one during a season of succession. Satan will stop at nothing to destroy unity in the body of Christ, particularly when senior leaders are in transition. The church could be thought of as Ground Zero.

The Pentagon is the world's largest office complex. It is home to the leadership of our military's five branches (i.e., the Navy, Army, Marines, Air Force, and Coast Guard), and an estimated twenty-three thousand people work there. In the center of the complex, there is an open commons area with lawn, sidewalks and benches that the staff has aptly nicknamed Ground Zero. Why Ground Zero? Our military intelligence has determined that a majority of the nuclear missiles of our enemies are aimed at the Pentagon. Hence, this one spot in our country is "Ground Zero". Our enemies have reasoned that if they eliminate our military leaders, they have every greater chance of conquering our nation. In a similar fashion, our enemy has reasoned that if he takes out the leaders of the church, he has every greater chance of conquering one congregation after another. During a leader><shift, the transitioning pastors, staff, and key leaders are wearing proverbial targets on their backs. They are in the crosshairs of the enemy who opposes the body of Christ. As we read in Scripture, we must "resist the devil and stand firm in the faith" (1 Peter 5:9), for "greater is He who is in us, than he who is in the world" (1 John 4:4).

Succession is not about the personalities of two men, but it is about the person of Jesus Christ. Succession is not about giving honor to the exiting leader or searching for a rising star personality so much as it is about advancing the kingdom of God and keeping Jesus Christ as the famous one. All too often, the church or parachurch organization will lose focus on the spiritual dimension of succession, and when that happens, we fail to "fix our eyes on Jesus, the author and perfecter of our faith" (Hebrews 12:2). We must make every effort to pursue and maintain sincere, profound spirituality throughout the succession process.

One way to do so is to keep people praying. Develop ways to foster a prayerful environment among the entire community of believers with regard to succession. Send out e-updates with items needing prayer. In worship gatherings, pray together for God to be honored in a succession that is first and foremost devoted to bringing glory to Him. When in meetings involving succession, pray not only at the beginning, but at different and appropriate times throughout the meeting—and then close the meeting with prayer. It is appropriate to declare a church-wide time of praying and fasting for God's will to be made known in the succession process. It is essential to not only communicate with one another at deeper levels, but it is all the more important to communicate with God at the deepest of all levels in prayer. Dietrich Bonhoeffer described prayer in the church as an essential to spiritual and community life.

> "A Christian fellowship lives and exists by the intercession of its members for one another, or it collapses. I can no longer condemn or hate a brother for whom I pray, no matter how much trouble he causes me. His face, that hitherto may have been strange and intolerable to me, is transformed in intercession into the countenance of a brother for whom Christ died, the face of a forgiven sinner. This is a happy discovery for the Christian who begins to pray for others."[85]

Prayer does not happen naturally; so we must intentionally engage in intercession, both fervently and frequently when we find ourselves in the midst of succession. The night before His death on the cross, Jesus prayed for His disciples and for "those who will believe in me through their message, that all of them may be one..." (John 17:20-21). He went on to pray: "May they be brought to complete unity to let the world know that you sent me and have loved them even as

---

[85] Dietrich Bonhoeffer, *Life Together* (New York: Harper & Row Publishers, 1954), p. 86.

you have loved me" (John 17:23). Jesus prayed for our unity, and we should do the same. When in the midst of transition, pray for unity among all people in the church. While in the season of a succession, pray for God's will in heaven to be done here on earth: nothing more, nothing less, nothing else.

Push pause.

If the ministry you lead is advancing the kingdom of God, you are a threat to Satan. Describe the methods you are using to resist his attacks, particularly during your leadership transition. How important is prayer to you, your leadership team, and to your community of believers? How are you specifically interceding for one another in this time of succession?

EPILOGUE

People do not remember how we came into the ministry;
they remember how we left.

It is my hope that something I have written has caused you to think about the leader><shift yet to take place in your future. The pause points throughout the book should cause us to listen and watch for the promptings of God in our thinking. Elijah was at a significant moment in his life when God spoke to him in a quiet whisper (1 Kings 19:12-13), and not in the loud winds of a storm. God, who is forever the same, can—and will—speak to us when we sincerely seek Him. We need those moments of sensing God's quiet whisper, as He directs our paths in the final season of leadership. When the disciples of Jesus were so busy that they did not have time to eat, Jesus invited them to "come with Me by yourselves to a quiet place and get some rest' (Mark 6:31). There comes a time when we must pause from the frenetic pace of ministry to draw close to God in hopes of hearing His quiet whisper. After all, this is about finishing strong.

The year 1945 was a great year for rookie evangelists. In that year, twenty-seven year old Billy Graham came out of nowhere and was filling auditoriums across America, speaking to as many as 30,000 people a night. He was the first full-time evangelist for Youth for Christ, and before he finished his life-long ministry, he preached to over 250 million people in stadiums around the world, and to hundreds of millions more via television. Still, in 1945, there were two other young preachers filling auditoriums across America. One was a friend of Billy Graham's and his name was Charles Templeton, who preached to thousands and was called "the next Babe Ruth of evangelism." As well, twenty-five year old Bron Clifford began preaching across America in 1945, along with Graham and Templeton. In that year, he preached to thousands in Miami, where people would stand in line just hoping to get a seat. He preached in chapel at Baylor University and the president ordered all of the class bells to be turned off so as not to interrupt the preaching. All three young men were leading great numbers of people to Christ.

Most of us know the rest of the story, at least with regard to Billy Graham, but what about Templeton and Clifford? Charles Templeton left the ministry and Christianity. He even wrote a book entitled *Farewell to God: My Reasons for Rejecting the Christian Faith* (McClelland & Steward, 1996). Just nine years into his ministry, in a battle with alcohol and financial irresponsibility, Bron Clifford walked away from his ministry, his wife, his two children, and at the young age of thirty-five, he died of cirrhosis of the liver in a run-down motel outside of Amarillo, Texas. Of three strong, influential men of God, two did not finish well.[86]

Will that be said of us? As we near the end of our ministry, will only one out of three of us finish strong? What can we do to beat the odds? What can we do to increase our chance of finishing strong as followers of Jesus Christ? Think of it this way. Having run some marathons, there were a few things that I had to focus on in order to finish—and finish

---

[86] Steve Farrar, *Finishing Strong*. (Sisters, OR: Multnomah Books; 1995), pp. 3-5.

strong. These five essential issues are pace, intake, strength, companionship and focus.

- **Pace**: I have to keep a right pace or I will become exhausted too early in the marathon and not have enough strength to finish.
- **Intake**: I have to keep drinking and eating while running 26.2 miles.
- **Strength**: I must have some inner core physical strength from having trained and prepared as it takes inner core strength to finish a marathon.
- **Companion(s)**: I can be encouraged by running with other people because we are able to urge one another on to the finish, and speaking of finish…
- **Focus**: I must stay focused on the finish. It is easy to get distracted and discouraged by the mileage signs along the roadside in a marathon: "mile one", "mile two," etc. To finish strong, I have to keep thinking of crossing the finish line—one step at a time.

If a runner pays attention to these five essentials, a strong finish is all the more likely. Moreover, the same is true for us as aging leaders in the body of Christ. If we pay close attention to these same five essentials, we have a greater likelihood of finishing strong.

- **Pace:** We need to pay attention to the pace at which we are doing life and ministry. Runners do not all run at the same pace, and we do not do life at the same pace as one another. Some can handle ministry when it is full and complicated, others cannot. But, each of us must pursue life at a good and right pace so that we do not fail to walk with God.

- **Intake:** Every day, we need to be taking in the Word of God. We need to nourish ourselves spiritually through prayer and His Word, particularly as we near the time of our own leader><shift. Without intentional spiritual intake, don't expect to finish strong. Jesus said, "Apart from Me you can do nothing" (John 15:5). Without Christ, we can't finish strong. Not once, but three times, Jesus called Himself the "bread of life" and we must nourish ourselves by walking in deep communion with Christ.

- **Strength:** Our real strength is in the Holy Spirit. We need His counsel as we near the end of our ministry path. We need His strength to endure the unique temptations associated with handing over our ministry responsibilities to someone younger and more capable than are we. God is spirit—He is without skin (John 4:24); Jesus is God with skin on (John 1:14); yet the Holy Spirit is God in our skin (1 Corinthians 6:19). Just as a marathoner must have inner core strength, we must have the indwelling strength of the Holy Spirit at the core of our being if we hope to finish well.

- **Companion(s):** To finish strong, we need one another. As Christian leaders, we do life well when they do life with one another in authentic, Christ-centered community. Even Jesus called on others to help Him finish well. The night before His execution, Jesus was in the Garden of Gethsemane where He said to His eleven disciples, "Stay here and keep watch with Me." Jesus reached out to others for help when nearing His finish line, and we must do the same.

- **Focus:** Stay focused on the finish! The Apostle Paul did. Even though he was imprisoned, shipwrecked, savagely beaten, left for dead and more; there came a time when he was on death-row and he said, "The time of my departure has come. I have fought the good fight, I have finished the race, I have kept the faith. Now there is in store for me the crown of righteousness, which the Lord, the righteous Judge, will award to me on that day — and not only to me, but also to all who have longed for his appearing" (2 Timothy 4:6-8). Stay focused on finishing strong.

It was Monday night, August 3, at the 1992 Olympics in Barcelona, Spain. At the track and field stadium, the gun sounded for the 400-meter semifinals. Shortly into the race, Britain's Derek Redmond fell to the track with a torn right hamstring. Medical attendants rushed out to assist him, but as they approached Redmond, he waved them off while struggling to his feet. He crawled and then hopped in a desperate effort to finish the race. Though many people remember this Olympic moment, many people are unaware that just four years earlier, Redmond had also qualified for the 1988 Olympics in Seoul, Korea. Ninety seconds before his heat in 1988, he had to pull out of the Olympics because of Achilles tendon problems. Following that injury, Redmond underwent five surgeries and was able to qualify again for the 1992 Olympics. Yet, it happened again, but this time, it was a career ending injury.

Derek Redmond was determined to finish the race. As he worked his way towards the finish line, the television camera caught the sight of a man pushing aside a security guard as he came running onto the track. The determined person was Jim Redmond, Derek's father. Jim was one of those sports dads who changed his whole life for the sake of his athletic son. He changed jobs; and he often had a change of address, moving from place to place in order to find the best training for his son. With his arm around his son's waist, and Derek's arm around his dad's shoulder, they continued down the track towards the finish line. Thousands watching from the stands jumped to their feet and applauded Redmond, cheering him on to the finish—and that is just what he did—he finished what his nation had sent him to do.

We belong to a sending God. He sent you and me to lead, and now as we approach the end of our event, we must finish strong. Just as Jim Redmond helped his son finish what he had been sent to do, our Father does the same. He is at our side helping us to be faithful to the finish. What matters to God is that we stay faithful. Nowhere in the Bible does God call us to be successful. Jesus said, "Be faithful, even to the point of death, and I will give you the crown of life" (Rev. 2:10b).

Stay faithful. Finish strong.